Virgo
24 August – 23 September

DID YOU PURCHASE THIS BOOK WITHOUT A COVER?
If you did, you should be aware it is **stolen property** as it was reported *unsold and destroyed* by a retailer. Neither the author nor the publisher has received any payment for this book.

All Rights Reserved including the right of reproduction in whole or in part in any form. This edition is published by arrangement with Harlequin Enterprises II B.V./S.à.r.l. The text of this publication or any part thereof may not be reproduced or transmitted in any form or by any means, electronic or mechanical, including photocopying, recording, storage in an information retrieval system, or otherwise, without the written permission of the publisher.

This book is sold subject to the condition that it shall not, by way of trade or otherwise, be lent, resold, hired out or otherwise circulated without the prior consent of the publisher in any form of binding or cover other than that in which it is published, and without a similar condition including this condition being imposed on the subsequent purchaser.

® and ™ are trademarks owned and used by the trademark owner and/or its licensee. Trademarks marked with ® are registered with the United Kingdom Patent Office and/or the Office for Harmonisation in the Internal Market and in other countries.

First published in Great Britain 2009
by Harlequin Mills & Boon Limited,
Eton House, 18-24 Paradise Road, Richmond, Surrey TW9 1SR

Copyright © Dadhichi Toth 2008 & 2009

ISBN: 978 0 263 87069 5

Typeset at Midland Typesetters Australia

Harlequin Mills & Boon policy is to use papers that are natural, renewable and recyclable products and made from wood grown in sustainable forests. The logging and manufacturing processes conform to the legal environmental regulations of the country of origin.

Printed and bound in Spain
by Litografia Rosés S.A., Barcelona

About
Dadhichi

Dadhichi is one of Australia's foremost astrologers. He has the ability to draw from complex astrological theory to provide clear, easily understandable advice and insights for people who want to know what their future might hold.

In the 26 years that Dadhichi has been practising astrology, face reading and other esoteric studies, he has conducted over 9,500 consultations. His clients include celebrities, political and diplomatic figures, and media and corporate identities from all over the world.

Dadhichi's unique blend of astrology and face reading helps people fulfil their true potential. His extensive experience practising western astrology is complemented by his research into the theory and practice of eastern systems of astrology.

Dadhichi features in numerous newspapers and magazines and he also appears regularly on many of Australia's leading television and radio networks, where many of his political and worldwide forecasts have proved uncannily accurate.

His website www.astrology.com.au is now one of the top ten online Australian lifestyle sites and, in conjunction with www.facereader.com, www.soulconnector.com and www.psychjuice.com, they attract over half a million visitors monthly. The websites offer a wide variety of features, helpful information and personal services.

Dedicated to The Light of Intuition
Sri V. Krishnaswamy — mentor and friend
With thanks to Julie, Joram, Isaac and Janelle

Welcome from Dadhichi

Dear Friend,

Welcome! It's great to have you here, reading your horoscope, trying to learn more about yourself and what's in store for you in 2010.

I visited Mexico a while ago and stumbled upon the Mayan prophecies for 2012, which, they say, is the year when the longstanding calendar we use in the western world supposedly stops! If taken literally, some people could indeed believe that 'the end of the world is near'. However, I see it differently.

Yes, it might seem as though the world is getting harder and harder to deal with, especially when fear enters our lives. But, I believe that 'the end' indicated by these Mayan prophecies has more to do with the end that will create new beginnings for our societies, more to do with making changes to our material view of life and some necessary adjustments for the human race to progress and prosper in future. So let's get one thing straight: you and I will both be around after 2012, reading our 2013 horoscopes!

My prediction and advice centres around keeping a cool mind and not reacting to the fear that could overtake us. Of course, this isn't easy, especially when media messages might increase our anxiety about such things as the impacts of global warming or the scarcity of fossil fuels.

I want you to understand that it is certainly important to be aware and play your part in making the world a better place; however, the best and surest way to support global goals is to help yourself first. Let me explain. If everyone focused just a little more on improving *themselves* rather than just pointing their finger to criticise others, it would result in a dramatic change and improvement; not just globally, but societally. And, of course, you mustn't forget what a positive impact this would have on your personal relationships as well.

Astrology focuses on self-awareness; your own insights into your personality, thinking processes and relationships. This is why this small book you have in your hand doesn't only concentrate on what is going to happen, but more importantly how you can *make* things happen positively through being your best.

I have always said that there are two types of people: puppets and actors. The first simply react to each outside stimulus and are therefore slaves of their environment, and even of their own minds and emotions. They are puppets in the hands of karma. The other group I call actors. Although they can't control what happens to them all the time, either, they are better able to adapt and gain something purposeful in their lives. They are in no way victims of circumstance.

I hope you will use what is said in the following pages to become the master of your destiny, and not rely on the predictions that are given as mere fate but as valuable guidelines to use intelligently when life presents you with its certain challenges.

Neither the outside world, nor the ups and downs that occur in your life, should affect your innermost spirituality and self-confidence. Take control: look beyond your current challenges and use them as the building blocks of experience to create success and fulfilment in the coming year.

I believe you have the power to become great and shine your light for all to see. I hope your 2010 horoscope book will be a helpful guide and inspiration for you.

Warm regards, and may the stars shine brightly for you in 2010!

Your Astrologer,

Dadhichi Toth

Contents

The Virgo Identity 11

   Virgo: A Snapshot 13

Star Sign Compatibility 33

2010: The Year Ahead 65

2010: Month By Month Predictions 79

   January 81

   February 86

   March 91

   April 96

   May 101

   June 106

July 111

August 116

September 121

October 126

November 131

December 136

2010: Astronumerology 141

2010: Your Daily Planner 169

VIRGO

The Virgo Identity

THE VIRGO IDENTITY

Try not to become a man of success but a man of value.

—Albert Einstein

Virgo: A Snapshot

Key Characteristics

Analytical, reserved, selfless, introverted, exacting, perfectionist, critical

Compatible Star Signs

Taurus, Capricorn, Cancer, Scorpio

Key Life Phrase

I serve

Life Goals

To create works of excellence that also inspire others

Platinum Assets

Selfless service, intuitive mind, tireless work ethic

Zodiac Totem

The Virgin

Zodiac Symbol

♍

Zodiac Facts

Sixth sign of the zodiac; mutable, barren, feminine, dry

Element

Earth

Famous Virgos

Sean Connery, Macaulay Culkin, Shania Twain, Michael Jackson, Cameron Diaz, Keanu Reeves, Charlie Sheen, Beyonce Knowles, Adam Sandler, Hugh Grant, Ryan Phillippe, Rachel Ward, David Copperfield, Jada Pinkett Smith, Sophia Loren, Bill Murray, Luke Wilson, Nicole Richie, Ricki Lake, Stephen King

Virgo: Your profile

Life isn't a dress rehearsal, or so most Virgos believe. You see, you don't like leaving anything to chance and are diligent with everything you do. There's no cutting corners if you're a Virgo. The desire to perfect your actions, serve others and to live a noble life is at the heart of your Virgo personality.

As a typical Virgo, you are constantly trying to improve things, both in yourself and others. As a consequence, you are misunderstood by others who believe you are simply being critical for the sake of it. Unfortunately, they don't see just how tough you are on yourself and that you extend these rigorous standards to your own life, not just to the lives of others. Because you believe in first-class service, you want to be the best you can and usually see where others can also excel in being their best, too.

THE VIRGO IDENTITY

At times you are a hard taskmaster, difficult to please and, if you're one of the less-sensitive Virgos among your zodiac sign, you could be rather ruthless when it comes to giving your so-called 'constructive' criticism. You cut through to the heart of the problem but often run roughshod over other people's feelings, so much so that you don't necessarily improve them. You need to be more careful of this harsh trait.

Most Virgos I meet are particularly fastidious and hygienic in every aspect of their lives. You can easily spot the Virgo environment. Everything is in its place. Even books on shelves are preferably placed in order of size and thickness so that everything is neatly detailed and categorised. You hate dirt, dust and other types of messiness; although there is the odd Virgo individual who is the complete opposite and is very untidy, but this is quite rare.

In the extreme, some Virgos become compulsive about cleanliness and keeping healthy, and do not let anything interfere with their wellbeing or physical vitality. This may cause them to avoid others or to take cleanliness to extraordinary lengths. As a Virgo, try to relax and understand that not everyone has the same values as you do. It's quite unlikely you are going to contract some dreaded disease simply by shaking hands with someone.

Virgo has very balanced speech and likes to express understanding through communication. This makes you an excellent confidant and adviser to friend and stranger alike. You have the ability to

VIRGO

think outside the square and help others through your in-built desire to serve, which is the main theme of the star sign of Virgo. You have a broad mind, a particularly big heart, and like to make others feel good, even if at times you do come across as critical. Mostly, people will see through this and understand that your motivations are honourable and therefore you draw people to you through trust and honour.

Your Virgo mind is a deep and analytical one. You are not interested in superficialities and this includes your relationships. You like a challenge and anyone who is a complex individual will meet that challenge perfectly for you. You are attracted to them because you like to understand the ins and outs of the human mind.

Always on the cutting edge of learning, you are the eternal student looking to broaden your horizons and understand as much of life as you can. Self-understanding is also included in this lifelong study.

You are a very principled person and pride yourself on honesty but also expect others to reciprocate this quality in their friendship with you. You never short-change anyone and give more than you receive. At times this will be a burden because deep down you would love to feel that you are worthy of love and service in the same way that you offer this to those nearest and dearest to you.

Being a shy, introverted type of individual you must come out of your shell and ask for your needs to be met. Don't be afraid to make your feelings known. Others will appreciate your openness.

Three classes of Virgo

Most Virgos don't like to be in the limelight but this is more pronounced in those of you who are born between the 24th of August and the 3rd of September. You absolutely hate being singled out in a group. This is probably one of your pet fears. Remaining anonymous doesn't bother you and you're quite happy to work away at your own pace doing what you do best—which is simply excellent work.

If you were born between the 4th and the 14th of September you have a rather unique mind and your intelligence is of a high order. You have the knack of understanding even complex problems. You're intuitive and quick off the mark when it comes to seizing opportunities in life. Try not to be too serious and enjoy the energies of Mercury, your ruling planet, which is humorous and playful.

You are young at heart if you were born between the 15th and the 23rd of September. The planet co-ruling you is Venus and brings with it charm, zest and a youthful appearance. Even in old age people will marvel at how well you have 'preserved' yourself. Not only that, you have a fun sense of humour that others find infectious.

Virgo role model: Michael Jackson

Even though there is little doubt Michael Jackson is a rather quirky figure, you have to hand it to

VIRGO

him: he showcases the kind of perfectionism that is typical of the Virgo personality. With an undeniably amazing dedication to his craft of dancing, music and entertainment, he reflects Virgo's brilliance completely.

Virgo: The light side

Very few people understand just how loyal you are, Virgo. The difficulty could be that you are a shy and retiring type of individual and don't necessarily show your hand too soon in a friendship. It takes a little while for others to realise just how dedicated you are in love.

In this day and age, people usually have some ulterior motive when they offer some form of help. You would have to be forgiven for feeling a little reluctant to open your heart to the first person who comes along. At times you have offered your hand of friendship without any expectation of return only to be hurt. But this is precisely one of your most endearing qualities. You value friendship and live the ideal; you don't just pay lip service to it. You give unconditionally.

Your quick mind is full of ideas for improving things while also practically achieving your professional and financial objectives. You're able to convey your ideas through precise communication, so there is usually no ambiguity about what you mean. In this way you avoid disputes and, if for some reason someone challenges you, you're quick in pointing out the error of their ways and do this in a diplomatic way.

You see all sides of the situation clearly and even when people oppose you you're able to fairly present your side of the story. Therefore, Virgo, you could be called a peacemaker.

Virgo: The shadow side

The hardest thing for you to do is observe a problem or error and not do anything about it. You're just not wired that way. But that isn't the main problem. It's the manner in which you go about rectifying the problem when you have to point out a fault to others. Constructive criticism is one thing, but you can be, and usually are, quite sharp in the way you present these criticisms.

You push yourself hard, sometimes too hard, and this can result in a lack of sleep, continual worry and self-deprivation. You never feel as if your best is good enough, so you always take yet another step further towards perfection. Your happiness might prove elusive because you continually postpone inner satisfaction by finding fault with yourself.

Don't let cleanliness become a fastidious habit. Some obsessive-compulsive people are born under Virgo, which can be seen even from a young age. The most important key to your happiness is relaxation and letting others be. This will go a long way to fulfilling you in life.

Virgo woman

Women born under the sign of Virgo are graceful, gentle and shy by nature. But this is not an invitation to take advantage of them. By no means! The grace and sweetness found in women of your star sign is only one of your unique strengths.

You have a powerful mind and are not scared to voice your opinions once you are clear about the social terrain and comfortable enough with the people you are dealing with. In fact, once you do put forward your views, people are rather surprised at the power behind your opinions.

Mercury is the ruler of your star sign and gives you incredible communication skills. You are observant, methodical and clear in your understanding of any situation. If people feel you lack imagination, so be it. You would prefer to be in control of what's happening rather than living in an airy-fairy dream state.

In this way you are able to solve your problems and are not afraid to do this alone without the support of others. Indeed, you pride yourself on independence and a capacity to stand your ground in life, even when the going gets tough. You have persistence and a strong moral compass.

You are especially loyal to your friends even though you may not have many because, to you, the world is not overly replete with genuine characters. Finding a true friend is often much like finding a needle in a haystack according to your Virgoan philosophy.

THE VIRGO IDENTITY

You're able to do an incredible amount of work due to the fact that you are a genuine multi-tasker. If you want something done, give it to a Virgo woman. You have a knack of squeezing several extra dozen hours into a day and people wonder how you do this. Chalk it up to your incredibly agile mind.

Humour is also one of your better traits. Others are attracted to it and, if you develop this particular character trait to a greater degree, it might just help you bypass some of the highly strung elements of your personality. By overworking, by trying to be a superwizz and doing way too much, you run the risk of damaging your health and forever postponing essential 'me time'. Be good to yourself; you deserve it.

Because service comes so easily to you, you'll naturally aspire to a family life, marriage and rearing children. Taking care of each and every need of your loved ones will be a pleasure and this will be one of the most fulfilling areas of your life. You are very idealistic about family and need someone who will share your ideals of service and impeccable loyalty.

Choosing friends may be difficult for you at times because of your very high standards. You pride yourself on the company you keep and can in no way handle anything crude or low class. Women born under Virgo are very frugal but nonetheless are able to dress and present themselves in a very tasteful way. You are not a show-off and come across as a humble individual.

Virgo man

Virgo men are an enigma, to say the least. You probably find that others don't quite know where you're coming from, and this can be attributed to your ruling planet Mercury, which is a changeable and tricky sort of influence for those born under its energies. Now, because you have understood this fact, you can actually use it to your advantage. You appreciate that, when people don't quite grasp who you are and what your motives might be, you exert more power and control in life.

You are perceptive, quick-witted and able to grasp clearly what others are thinking and doing. In some ways you have a psychic ability, but not in a clairvoyant way. This is more likely a type of intellectual insight that is so quick even your mind may not grasp the power you have over others. Use this wisely.

You're an inquisitive sort of person and like to explore life and all of the possibilities available to you. You never stop learning and pride yourself on your intellectual abilities. You love a good discussion and, even if you're out of your depth in the company of experts, you somehow understand almost instinctively what they are discussing and can usually contribute something, even if it's not on an authoritative level.

There are two distinct sides of your nature, and friends and family see this in you. One side of your personality is forever hidden and you like it that

THE VIRGO IDENTITY

way. Although you are calm, reserved and sometimes silent on many matters, there is a passionate side of your character that is surprising to your friends. You can turn it off and on at will. You like to reveal the fullness of your character only to those whom you choose and trust.

Mostly you prefer to express your love in staid, practical ways. You may need to change this a little because women prefer demonstrativeness and affection. This is not to say you aren't a sensual individual, but your basic drive is to look after the practical, security issues of the ones you love.

Being born under Virgo means you have a love of perfection and need to express yourself through good work and successful enterprises. This is no less evident in your personal life, around the home, in your most ordinary moments and as well as in your professional life. You believe that if the job is to be done, it should be done to the best of your ability so that it expresses the best in you. Because of this you are valued as a contributor in your personal and career lives and will be successful in any line you choose.

Virgo child

As long as you give a Virgo child plenty of mental stimulation, it should keep them out of trouble. Creative, inquisitive and brilliant intellectually by nature, you learn very soon that your little Virgo baby is no ordinary mortal. But be careful of this because it will be very easy to treat them as if they

VIRGO

are some sort of superman or superwoman, which will place an immense amount of pressure on them from an early age.

This is why some children born under Virgo become exceedingly worrisome about their abilities, how they look, and whether or not everything is going to be okay in life. It is up to you to let them live their lives as children before placing an undue burden on them to be better than they are. Teach them how to have fun, how to express the creative side of their personalities, which they have in abundance.

Being highly strung by nature, it's a good idea to teach them the value of sport, outdoor activities and adequate rest. Because of their overly active minds they will have the tendency to stay up late and become overtired. This will create a vicious cycle that makes them feel worse day by day. If you pay attention to their daily schedule, helping them eat properly, think creatively and play joyfully, they will grow up to be balanced people.

Virgo children hate to be disturbed by stress, arguments or confrontation. It could be disastrous if your little Virgoan child is growing up in an atmosphere of dispute and tension. They will soon let you know if they're not happy, however, and this could be an excellent barometer of your own relationship with your partner. Try to foster peace and harmony in your home so that your Virgo child will grow up being happy and healthy.

At school Virgo may be a little shy in warming to others. Let them move at their own pace in making friends until they start to become accustomed to the environment and the types of people to whom they are being exposed.

Social life is an integral part of their character, but you also need to understand they enjoy their own company. They want to contemplate life and human nature, even though they seem a little too young for that sort of thing. Please, remember never to underestimate your Virgo child.

Romance, love and marriage

We mustn't misinterpret the pure and virginal symbol of Virgo by thinking they are averse to love, friendship and relationships. This analogy may have something more to do with the virginal, fertile mind of those born under your star sign. Certainly, you're not as quick as some of the other signs to come forward in expressing your feelings, but this doesn't mean you don't have a beautiful heart and a great deal to offer someone in a relationship.

You have the magnetic power to attract many sorts of people in life; but only a few of these will be of sufficiently high quality in your estimation to spend the rest of your life with. And you are quite happy to weed out these initial suitors by prodding and prying into their minds to find out what makes them tick. Thirty per cent won't make it to first base. 'Well and good,' you will say. 'I won't have to deal with them again, and good riddance.' You are fussy—and so you should be.

VIRGO

Another 30 per cent might find the first month or two a little too gruelling due to your exacting standards. You'd be the first to admit that you demand a lot from others and you are a critical perfectionist in what you want in love. That's okay, as long as you can take as well as you give.

This leaves 40 per cent. Most of these people will appreciate your honesty, your integrity and your ability to call a spade a spade. You don't embellish your thoughts. You don't have the typical exaggerative temperament of some of the other star signs. Some of these 40 per cent may find you a little boring; not because you are, but because they are so used to the sensationalism of romance.

Once you reduce these prospects in your love life down to a handful, you may be fortunate enough to find just a few gems who appreciate you for who you really are and what you bring to the table. You, Virgo, have an abundance of love and service-orientated drive to satisfy the right soulmate. With a smattering of humour and dedication to working on your relationship, the sometimes long and hard task of choosing someone from this handful and discarding the rest will all be worth it in the end.

You expect loyalty from your partner and can be rather vehement if you detect any sort of insincerity. To you, friendship is for keeps. Even if you happen to have differences of opinion, part of the joy of life for you is working through these differences and finding a common meeting ground. Compromise is one of your character traits, but not if it means ditching your morals. That area of your life is definitely off-limits when, and if, it comes to making concessions.

As with relationships on the whole, sexuality is a sacrosanct area for Virgo. This is probably more the case with women rather than men. Generally, however, you idealise love and see it is an almost spiritual bonding of two souls. The physical aspect of your relationship is never fulfilling enough if the intellectual component is missing. Neanderthals need not apply for a relationship with Virgo! If you feel confident that someone has covered all bases—mental, emotional, spiritual and physical—you'll have no problem sharing the deepest recesses of your soul with them.

Some Virgo-born individuals marry early. Mercury your ruler is indeed a young planet and shows that you will be aware of your sexuality at an early age. Once you understand what true love is really about, you'll persistently work hard to fulfil your dream of finding that perfect individual with whom you can share your life.

Once the trust of your partner is won, you'll show just how much fun you can be and that you are the type of person who wants to extract the most out of life. Simple things give you pleasure and you love to share these moments with your mate. This, to you, Virgo, is the stuff that real love is made of.

Health, wellbeing and diet

Of the zodiac signs, Virgo is the one which naturally rules health and so it stands to reason that,

VIRGO

by being born under this star sign, you will have a deep insight and sensitivity to issues of health and wellbeing.

Because Virgo is so sensitive, anything and everything can trigger reactions in your body. Environmental factors, poor diet, lack of sport, emotional dissatisfaction and poor sleep patterns contribute to complex health issues for you.

You have a tendency to worry about things, so your nervous system is one of the most important elements in keeping your body and mind fresh and healthy. Try to relax more and don't think to excess. If you have a problem, try to reason with yourself to understand that there are times when you are not going to find a solution right away. Work hard at letting go and trusting the universe to bring you the solution in its own good time.

Your digestive system will suffer not just from the food you eat but also from too much worry and overwork. Learn to listen to your body signals and shut down when it's time to rest. Get adequate downtime and listen to music as well as spend time in a quiet and relaxed atmosphere with those whom you feel comfortable. These are natural ways you can unwind and give your body the right sort of endorphins to create good health.

Smaller, more regular meals are in order for you, Virgo. You probably find yourself on the go most of the time and don't make the time to sit down and thoroughly chew your food. That's a no-no! You need to make time! If you start to feel the slightest niggle in your body, you'll probably blow it all out of proportion, so isn't it better to take the appropriate measures beforehand?

Calming herbs like skullcap, camomile, vervain and valerian root are ideally suited to the Virgo temperament and will help to bring you peace of mind. Always remember to include supplements such as Vitamins B, C and E, along with whole grains such as rye, wheat and barley in your diet. Of course, plenty of green vegetables will work wonders for you because Mercury, which rules the sign of Virgo, has a connection to green leafy vegetables.

Work

Success is easy for most Virgos and you shouldn't have too much trouble finding satisfaction through your work. Virgo being the sixth sign of the zodiac regulates employment, work and service, and so work is a natural fit for you.

Work is not something you do just to pass the time. You take it seriously and want to do your best. To you, work is not only about taking home your pay packet. You are not a clock-watcher and will diligently do what it takes to perfect your work and turn out the best quality in anything you do, even if it happens to be menial in the eyes of others.

You have an incredibly good executive ability and your organisational skills are excellent. You can manage people as well because you have a knack of communicating and mediating between different parties, sometimes with very diverse views. You're able to harmonise and stabilise your workforce if you are an employer and, if an employee, you have a sense of dedication and loyalty to those who give you opportunities in life.

Because you have such a deductive mind, careers which involve maths, logic, science and other intellectual skills will ideally suit your disposition. Problem solving, human relations, and dietetics or health-related fields could also fit comfortably with you as career choices.

Any line of customer service, irrespective of the industry, would serve you and your employers well because you have an in-built desire to provide satisfaction to your clients.

As long as you work in an environment that is conducive to a harmonious mental state and physical wellbeing, you should perform well and, slowly but surely, you will achieve your goal of success.

Key to karma, spirituality and emotional balance

Service is by far your main focus and the key words 'I serve' shine through everything you do. However, you must learn that another primary spiritual need is also to serve yourself and look after some of your own emotional desires.

Being analytical may be overemphasised in your life, so try to get in touch with your inner feelings and in this way your intuitive life will shine as well. Meditation and self-analysis on Wednesdays and

Saturdays will be conducive to a rewarding spiritual progress.

Your lucky days

Your luckiest days are Wednesdays, Fridays and Saturdays.

Your lucky numbers

Remember that the forecasts given later in the book will help you optimise your chances of winning. Your lucky numbers are:

5, 14, 23, 32, 41, 50

6, 15, 24, 33, 42, 51

8, 17, 26, 35, 44, 53

Your destiny years

Your most important years are 5, 14, 23, 32, 41, 50, 68, 77 and 86.

VIRGO

Star Sign Compatibility

The more a man knows, the more he forgives.

—Catherine the Great

Romantic compatibility

How compatible are you with your current partner, lover or friend? Did you know that astrology can reveal a whole new level of understanding between people simply by looking at their star sign and that of their partner? In this chapter I'd like to share some special insights that will help you better appreciate your strengths and challenges using Sun sign compatibility.

The Sun reflects your drive, willpower and personality. The essential qualities of two star signs blend like two pure colours, producing an entirely new colour. Relationships, similarly, produce their own emotional colours when two people interact. The following is a general guide to your romantic prospects with others and how, by knowing the astrological 'colour' of each other, the art of love can help you create a masterpiece.

When reading the following I ask you to remember that no two star signs are ever *totally* incompatible. With effort and compromise, even the most 'difficult' astrological matches can work. Don't close your mind to the full range of life's possibilities! Learning about each other and ourselves is the most important facet of astrology.

Each star sign combination is followed by the elements of those star signs and the result of

VIRGO

Quick-reference guide: Horoscope compatibility between signs (percentage)

	Aries	Taurus	Gemini	Cancer	Leo	Virgo	Libra	Scorpio	Sagittarius	Capricorn	Aquarius	Pisces
Aries	60	65	65	65	90	45	70	80	90	50	55	65
Taurus	60	70	70	80	70	90	75	85	50	95	80	85
Gemini	70	70	75	60	80	75	90	60	75	50	90	50
Cancer	65	80	60	75	70	75	60	95	55	45	70	50
Leo	90	70	80	70	85	70	65	75	95	45	70	90
Virgo	45	90	75	75	75	70	80	85	70	95	50	75
Libra	70	75	90	60	65	80	80	85	80	85	50	70
Scorpio	80	85	60	95	75	85	85	90	85	65	60	95
Sagittarius	90	50	75	55	95	70	80	80	85	55	60	75
Capricorn	50	95	50	45	45	95	85	65	55	85	70	85
Aquarius	55	80	90	70	70	50	95	60	60	70	80	55
Pisces	65	85	50	90	75	70	50	95	75	85	55	80

their combining. For instance, Aries is a fire sign and Aquarius is an air sign and this combination produces a lot of 'hot air'. Air feeds fire and fire warms air. In fact, fire requires air. However, not all air and fire combinations work. I have included information about the different birth periods within each star sign and this will throw even more light on your prospects for a fulfilling love life with any star sign you choose.

Good luck in your search for love, and may the stars shine upon you in 2010!

Compatibility quick-reference guide

Each of the twelve star signs has a greater or lesser affinity with one another. The quick-reference guide will show you who's hot and who's not so hot as far as your relationships are concerned.

VIRGO + ARIES
Earth + Fire = Lava

There's no point beating around the bush, Virgo. The bottom line is that you and Aries are not particularly compatible. Your ruling planets—Mercury and Mars, respectively—are not at all friendly in the astrological scheme of things and your elements, being earth and fire, do not gel particularly well, either. In other words, a relationship between the two of you will be an uphill battle from the start.

Your mentality is rooted in the idea of service, perfectionism and meticulous forethought. Aries,

VIRGO

however, is diametrically opposed to these traits, being fast, furious and impulsive. You are more reserved in the way you approach life and Aries' irritable and quick-moving nature bothers you in more ways than one.

You are more likely to control your impatience and your displeasure of others, but Aries will be quick to lash out when they feel too stifled by your slower, more circumspect ways. You like to take your time and analyse every angle before moving forward. This would essentially be the main sticking point in a relationship between the two of you.

Actually, because you're so well rounded, you are able to bring some value to a relationship with Aries, but they may be so busy doing so many things they may easily overlook the fact.

Aries does, however, have an exciting sort of lifestyle that stimulates you and makes you secretly wish you could be freer and more like them. A more patient type of Aries partner could at times help you express yourself more easily and encourage you to be a little less highly strung, for which Virgo is very well-known.

Passionate Aries will do everything it can to stimulate the playful side of your Virgo nature. But you do need time to get to know Aries and to feel more intimate. Aries is much more gung-ho and often not tactful enough for your refined lovemaking style. You also want communication, not just sex. That's not to say that Arians don't talk, because they do. But you would like to believe that what they do say has more depth and is not one-track minded.

Teaming up with an Aries born between the 21st and the 30th of March will result in more of a sexual affair than anything else. They have a very strong physical and passionate nature to which you will quickly have to adapt. Financial matters could work well between you.

A good relationship is likely between you and an Aries born between the 31st of March and the 10th of April. One thing, however, is that they are rather self-opinionated and don't handle criticism too well. If you can control yourself and allow them to be themselves, this could develop into a better match.

You have a reasonably good relationship with Aries born between the 11th and the 20th of April because they are strongly linked to the planet Jupiter, which is connected to your marriage zone. There's plenty of attraction both ways, physically and intellectually. This is one group of Aries that might just make you feel comfortable.

VIRGO + TAURUS
Earth + Earth = Solid Ground

The Virgo and Taurus combination is one of the supreme matches of the zodiac. This is an elemental combination that works, so your relationship with Taurus will feel comfortable from day one. It's a relationship that can satisfy both of you emotionally, physically and psychologically.

VIRGO

The earth signs such as yours and Taurus are well suited to the practical and material affairs of life, therefore you resonate easily with each other's needs. Because material security and financial satisfaction is a motivating force in both of your personalities, you'll instinctively feel as though your lives are destined to travel in the same direction together.

There's a considerable amount of comfort between the two of you, mainly because these ideals are so similar. Mutual security is so important in your relationship and Taurus will offer you this.

You admire the fact that Taurus can put in those hard, long hours of work to do what needs to be done in terms of taking care of financial responsibilities and family life. In some ways, they reflect the perfectionism to which Virgo so much aspires. They are the plodders of the zodiac, however, and therefore you need to be patient with them. One thing, though: you'll be satisfied they don't cut corners and like to do things as well as you do.

There's a vibrant sort of communication between yourself and Taurus because you have very similar interests, including art, music and other creative activities. The positive thing is that even if you have slight differences in your personalities, there's enough of a common interest to keep you both together over the long term.

Romance is a powerful force between you and your sexual and intimate life will also be extremely mutually satisfying. There's a balance between communication, emotional and physical stimulation and, although you don't have a particularly strong spiritual link with Taurus, over time, this will naturally develop. Taurus is slow off the mark and will test your creative impulses between the sheets.

With Taureans born between the 21st and the 29th of April, you can expect some really fun times due to the fact that Venus, the planet of love, endows them with considerable sensuality. You should feel fulfilled in a relationship with them.

If you team up with someone born between the 30th of April and the 10th of May, Mercury, which is your ruling planet and also influences them, indicates a strong karmic link between you. There'll be an amazing amount of communication and common interests. You will definitely attain great satisfaction with this group of Taureans.

Those Taureans born between the 11th and the 21st of May could be a little staid for your liking. This is because Saturn, the reserved and slow planet of the zodiac, dominates their personalities to a large extent. Although this is not the best of matches for you with Taurus, they still have a strong sense of duty and you will admire this.

VIRGO + GEMINI
Earth + Air = Dust

You're both ruled by Mercury, the whiz-bang communication planet of the zodiac. Therefore, you will

VIRGO

never be at a loss for words and will be constantly stimulating each other's minds.

Mercury operates in a somewhat different manner in Virgo compared to Gemini. In you, Virgo, it causes you to look more deeply into a subject; whereas with Gemini, the need is for multi-level, multi-tasking variety. They have so much going on at any given time that they are prone to be distracted and this might annoy you, especially if you get the feeling that when you're talking to them, there's something more important or interesting around the corner in their minds.

The main link between Virgo and Gemini seems to be the domestic area of your lives. To Gemini, you could be a great anchor, giving them insight into the value of family life, raising children and developing a strong future together in a communal sense. For you, however, Gemini may also be one of those star signs that can really stimulate you professionally, giving you new hope and energy with a vision that you may have not had before.

Try not to corner Gemini or impose too many of your rigid regulations on their lifestyles. If you keep it light-hearted and flexible, they'll be more prone to come around to your way of thinking. And another thing: don't hit them with too many criticisms, no matter how constructive. Gemini is a very sensitive sign, even if their talk makes them seem otherwise.

Because the two of you are ruled by the mischievous Mercury, your love life and sexual relationship together should be playful, interactive and exciting. You can expect plenty of role playing with Gemini, which means that your sensual interactions together should develop over time. There'll be nothing boring about lovemaking with them, that's for sure.

It's hard to find a soulmate in life but you may just hit upon a perfect partner if they're born between the 22nd of May and the 1st of June. They are extremely well suited to your temperament, being stimulating socially as well as intellectually. Due to the extra dose of Mercurial humour, their personalities are endowed with fun.

A softer, more sensual breed of Gemini is born between the 2nd and the 12th of June. Relationships with them will be inspiring, sensual and fulfilling on many other levels as well. They have a good knack for money and therefore a business arrangement with them will also do well.

Choosing a relationship with Geminis born between the 13th and the 21st of June could provide you excitement but also a lot of unpredictability. You'll have to take the good with the bad with this group of Geminis. Expect to be challenged but also to experience some wonderful surprises with Geminis born between these dates.

VIRGO + CANCER
Earth + Water = Mud

Virgo and Cancer make great mates! The sensitivity you both exhibit means that this relationship is

VIRGO

destined to be more than just a physical or sexual interplay. Cancer is one of the genuinely caring and compassionate signs of the zodiac, being ruled by the element of water. Water and earth always blend well as far as relationships are concerned and the Virgo–Cancer match is no exception.

Friendship is the foundation upon which your relationship is built. If you feel as though you enjoy the company of your Cancerian friend, then this is a good omen and the prognosis for the future between you is very good, very stable and fulfilling on pretty much every level.

Spending time together in a social context will be the cornerstone of your companionship. All of your friends will support your relationship and such support will always be a recurring aspect of it. However, you both very much need your own space and your own 'me' time, too; that is, some quiet time to reflect upon your own individual needs.

You both realise you can positively influence each other, help each other grow and develop the deeper emotional and psychological aspects of your personalities. For this reason, we can say that Virgo and Cancer is also one of the more compatible combinations of the zodiac. There's a positive, up-beat aspect present within it and Cancer also offers you domestic stability and happiness.

Not everyone is perfect, though, Virgo, and therefore you'll have to get used to Cancer's hypersensitive mood swings. You are quite critical—at times might I say scathing—in your comments and sometimes are not quite aware just how damaging this can be to someone like Cancer. Read the signals and you'll soon get a feel for how far you can take your criticisms. Use your knowledge to develop your level of intimacy and don't be so demanding of Cancer, especially in sexual matters.

Usually it's challenging to be both friend and lover to another person, but those in Cancer born between the 22nd of June and the 3rd of July are an exception. They make you feel great and you will also lift their spirits to a new high. Socially, you work well and will be surrounded by supportive friends. In the hard times, you can rely on each other as a bedrock of stability and emotional support.

Long-term love is possible with Cancer if they are born between the 14th and the 23rd of July. Your sexual compatibility also seems to be quite good, because they give you a sense of emotional satisfaction as well as physical enjoyment. You'll easily spend much time with them and deepen your awareness of things around you as a result.

With Cancerians born between the 4th and 13th of July, you can expect to meet a rather unusual type of character. They are spiritual, intuitive, highly sensitive and need to be handled with extra care. They may be more vulnerable than you would at first believe. You don't want to be treading on eggshells all your life, so you may want to study these characters a little first before committing to them.

VIRGO + LEO
Earth + Fire = Lava

Intellect and power. What a combination! And that's precisely what the Virgo–Leo romance is likely to revolve around. You, with your strong and inquisitive intellect, coupled with Leo's dramatic and somewhat arrogant style, will be a pretty hard match to ignore, wouldn't you say? The elements of earth and fire, your ruling elements, result in a 'hot' combination that is quite compelling but at the same time also very complex.

Leo will soon learn that Virgo is not as outgoing as they are and will quickly need to accommodate this fact. You're more prudent in sharing your feelings and less likely to want to be out in the limelight, which might cause problems for Leo, who not only likes to show off his or her own prowess but also likes to showcase their partner's as well. Perhaps you need to learn the art of acting to be able to walk arm in arm with your Leo partner on the world stage.

Leo is the dominant partner in this relationship, so you need to get used to this fact, even if you think you are more intellectually clever than they are, being a quite stubborn and fixed zodiac sign. And, furthermore, with your opinions and incessant need to improve things and point out the faults of others, you should expect to have continual run-ins with the self-opinionated and stubborn Leo. You'll have to use some very clever intellectual techniques to get a Leo to change.

STAR SIGN COMPATIBILITY

You lack the confidence that Leo exhibits and, if the truth be known, you can learn quite a bit from them in this respect. Many Virgos are shy and in some ways don't feel that what they have to say or to offer is of much value. Your Leo partner will soon shake that attitude out of you, making you feel generally more confident and self-assured about your ideas and yourself.

Leo is also an extremely loyal sign and this is something you will see very quickly in the relationship. They are generous with their love and their resources and you can't fault that in them. In the bedroom, Leo is a warm lover; but their fire is much more spontaneous than your own element of earth.

You're very attracted to Leos born between the 24th of July and the 4th of August. Somehow you don't feel quite as withdrawn as you do normally when you're in their company and are able to let go of your hang-ups. This makes you feel joyous and creatively fulfilled. You feel peaceful and confident with them.

A long-lasting relationship is likely if you team up with a Leo born between the 5th and the 14th of August. This is lucky for you emotionally and financially and the two of you can become wealthy as a couple. These Leos find you very attractive.

Leos born between the 15th and the 23rd of August are ruled by the dominant and argumentative Mars. This can be a problem for you when they try to exert their influence over the relationship. The tension between you is not going to make for a happy match.

VIRGO + VIRGO
Earth + Earth = Solid Ground

You'd better be prepared to take as good as you can give when it comes to meeting your star twin, Virgo. The two of you will mirror each other's personality and can be very demanding and critical of each other at times. Nevertheless, if you can accommodate these traits, common to both of you, there is a chance for the Virgo–Virgo match to endure.

You are perfectionists to a 'T' and you'll soon discover what it's like for other people to be on the receiving end of your criticisms and extremely high standards. Your Virgo partner will expect you to be up to par and this should be a good lesson for both of you. Try to keep it amiable and these criticisms will actually contribute to an improvement in the relationship.

Living with another Virgo will, for the most part, work well for you. Generally speaking, tidiness, cleanliness and hygiene are high on your agenda of what's essential in your partner. I can just imagine the pristine, almost flawlessly laid out house with spotlessly clean tiles, ceilings, furniture and neatly trimmed lawns.

Being earth signs, you're driven by your financial and professional success, and together you will encourage each other to do your best and achieve great heights. Your work philosophies follow similar lines and you are compassionate and supportive of each other's careers.

STAR SIGN COMPATIBILITY

Your home life is extremely important to both of you and creating a safe haven in which to express your genuine love and service to your loved ones will take on a special significance. Doing so together will give you a great deal of pleasure.

You are both tasteful and sensitive to each other's needs, intimately speaking, and your lovemaking will bring out the deeper aspects of your emotions. However, this may take time because you are both a little shy and uneasy about making physical contact too soon. But don't worry: over time you'll enjoy each other's company and will experience and explore the depths of sexuality.

Your best combination with Virgo is with those born between the 24th of August and the 2nd of September. You will mirror each other's insights and motivations very easily and each understands what turns the other on. The two of you are very much in sync with each other.

A serious relationship takes place if you choose to team up with Virgos born between the 3rd and the 12th of September. They like the finer things in life, so here's hoping you have a big enough bank balance to support that.

Getting involved with Virgos born between the 13th and the 23rd of September is a reasonably good match as well. Your destinies will collide and bring your relationship to a new level. This is due to the fact that Taurus and Venus are strongly linked to Virgos born on these dates.

VIRGO + LIBRA
Earth + Air = Dust

Virgo and Libra are an extremely good match but there are also some minor personality differences, which are well worth pointing out before you get too heavily involved with each other.

Mercury, your ruler, and Venus, the ruler of Libra, are excellent friends and this is a great start to the relationship. The combination of intellectual finesse and the charming persuasion of Venus works well, both in terms of your connection to each other and also as a unit in the world. These energies work to support you and bring you many friends and opportunities for success.

Libra has an extremely outgoing personality but is also sometimes rather indecisive in knowing what they want. You, Virgo, like the idea of careful planning and firm decision making that is based on a collection of the facts and figures and, once a decision is made, it's final. The approach of Libra in this respect may leave you frustrated. Libra has a tendency to change its mind; the scales of balance sway from side to side a little too often for your liking.

Regarding relationships, Libra has a tendency to want to play the field and is also much more flirtatious than you are. In the social context, you could find this a little upsetting, disheartening and even annoying. You'd like to feel as though your partner is 100 per cent committed to you and so you can expect moments of jealousy to well up within your heart if you are involved with Libra.

Sexuality and Libra go hand in hand. They are the sensual and romantic children of the zodiac and they love to please others. Therefore, you can expect to be well supported on a physical and sexual level by your Libran partner.

There are some differences you need to take note of, however, especially with those born between the 14th and the 23rd of October. You need to make quite a few compromises and concessions for these people because their personalities are rather outgoing and they are not partial to being tied down. This is due to the element of air that dominates them.

For a longer-lasting relationship, why not consider Librans born between the 4th and the 13th of October? They are not only sexually exciting, progressive and a little wacky, but a little more determined and grounded than the other Librans we are talking about. If you're prepared to try something new, do it with these Librans.

You feel loved and needed by Librans born between the 24th of September and the 3rd of October. They are the natural lovers of the zodiac who want to share their whole being with you. You see this as a form of reciprocal compassion and, therefore, you can expect to have a very good ongoing relationship with them.

VIRGO + SCORPIO
Earth + Water = Mud

It's only natural for your mind to seek out challenging intellectual circumstances and people. But what does this have to do with Scorpio, you ask? Well, the Scorpio personality is rich, fertile soil for your explorations into understanding yourself. You'll be biting off a challenging piece of wisdom if you choose to become involved with someone born under this zodiac sign.

The Scorpio character is deep, mysterious and most definitely attractive to you. They have a very powerful magnetic appeal and Virgo often finds this difficult to resist.

One other important factor is that friendship, based on mutual intellectual interests, provides both excitement, warmth and friendship between you.

You need to understand straight off that Scorpio is a very loyal sign and proud as well. You must never cross the line by breaching their trust, demeaning them or hurting their pride. You would pay a very high price for doing so.

On the other hand, if you honour your Scorpio partner, love them and share yourself completely, the rewards will be rich and long-lasting for your partnership.

Scorpio is a sexual sign and you'll need to have ample energy to fulfil this insatiable part of their nature. Physically speaking, the combination between you is good but Scorpio is more demanding in their needs and you need to learn the art of letting go and exploring some rather unusual highways and byways in the bedroom with them. Scorpio is the most sexual of the star signs and needs continual nourishment. This will be one of your biggest challenges in this relationship.

Scorpio is also one of the more dominant and sometimes sarcastic and critical signs of the zodiac. Your own critical mind will meet its match with your Scorpio partner. In fact, there could be a very subtle but friendly intellectual competitiveness that can develop in your relationship with them. But this is all good fun and can help you grow closer to each other and spiritually evolve, too.

With Scorpios born between the 24th of October and the 2nd of November, personality clashes are likely. They are intense characters but also demanding physically and emotionally. You mustn't try to analyse them too much psychologically or they could retaliate.

In your association with Scorpios born between the 3rd and the 12th of November, I can predict a very good outcome for your love lives and even possibly marriage. The planet Jupiter powerfully influences them and this planet dominates your marital affairs. This will be a natural fit for both of you and you'll feel that there is a strong link of destiny directing your lives together.

The group of Scorpios born between the 13th and the 22nd of November is emotionally difficult for you, Virgo. There is a tension about your association, and your finances will also not exactly work out together. You may want to get involved with them because most Scorpios attract you, but it's best to keep this partnership strictly on a business level. If you take the plunge and choose to go the full distance with them, make sure you are clear on your terms of engagement.

VIRGO + SAGITTARIUS
Earth + Fire = Lava

If you're the type of Virgo-born individual who demands honesty and integrity in your relationships, then you're likely to find it with Sagittarius. And there's very few Virgos that don't have very high ethical and moral standards, so this could apply to you.

But be warned: the honesty you seek will be handed to you bluntly, directly, and without any thought for your sensitivities. You are sometimes thin-skinned and may get more than you bargained for in the honesty stakes with your Sagittarian partner.

The Sagittarian is a large-hearted individual who loves freedom and mobility. Adventure is their second name and, therefore, this independent drive to be free may conflict with your need for more security and a well-ordered life. The Sagittarian is only partly compatible with you. Identifying your differences will be the first step in your relationship

STAR SIGN COMPATIBILITY

with them. Once that is ironed out, you can proceed to the next level.

Travel is important and this aspect of the relationship with Sagittarius might just work. They're curious on cultural and philosophical levels. Discussions centring around these topics will satisfy you, but you may be too rigid and critical and this may not sit well with the Sagittarian temperament.

The big challenge with Sagittarius is for you to let go of some of your preconceived ideas. When I talk about adventure with the Sagittarian character, I also talk about the exploration of the mind and ability to see beyond your self-limits. Sagittarius will challenge you in this regard and, if you're an evolved Virgo, you could learn some important lessons in your relationship with them.

You are fairly reserved in your approach to sexual matters, which is quite a contrast to the Sagittarian bravado. They are experimental in lovemaking and not quite as slow as you would prefer them to be. This, therefore, is also not the best combination for you sexually.

You can have a reasonably good relationship with Sagittarians born between the 23rd of November and the 1st of December. These individuals are probably your best choice in the Sagittarian group and they're enterprising spirit does attract you. Being natural travellers and explorers of the world, you can enjoy their company and learn a lot while trekking the globe together.

Tension and out-and-out war is likely with Sagittarians born between the 2nd and the 11th of December. This could be an argumentative combination, and take note that your health may be affected by your association with these people. By entering a relationship with Sagittarians born in this period, you do so at your own risk.

Sagittarians don't generally fulfil you and neither do those who are born between the 12th and the 22nd of December. But look a little deeper with these individuals, because there are some aspects that may interest you and give you cause for hope. You both enjoy meeting people from different cultures and philosophical persuasions, which could be the common meeting ground for the two of you.

VIRGO + CAPRICORN
Earth + Earth = Solid Ground

Because of your self-analytical disposition, it's likely a relationship with Capricorn will cause you both to think too much, particularly on some of the negative aspects of your lives. You need to keep this relationship up-beat or it could deteriorate into a 'woe is me' scenario.

Capricorn is ruled by Saturn, the tester, the hermit, the traditional and serious planet. Capricorn is down-to-earth, reliable and completely committed to security, which is something you admire in them. But emotionally and mentally, you need something between you that is going to lighten the relationship and make you both happy.

Capricorn will be a little surprised at your chatty nature and ability to identify aspects of their personality and motivations. Patience will be important because Capricorn doesn't move as quickly as you. You can take this to apply both to the practical affairs of life and also your physical relationship.

Give Capricorn some space to think and also to be alone because it's important for them to contemplate their strategies, their relationships, and what the overall meaning of life is to them. Don't push them in the relationship or you might scare them away. Trust that even if they do feel close to you and love you, they may not always be able to express it as easily as you do. You might take their silence and their somewhat solemn moods to be a rejection of your overtures. This isn't the case and in time, if you persist, you'll realise just how loyal and loving your Capricorn partner can be.

If you join hands with a Capricorn born between the 11th and the 20th of January, you can expect a blue ribbon relationship with them. This is a powerfully compatible combination due to the fact that Mercury has a strong rulership over these individuals and is your ruling planet, too. This is one of those combinations that will go the full-term and may even offer you excellent marital prospects.

Those Capricorn individuals born between the 23rd of December and the 1st of January work well with you on many levels. There's also a great financial and material compatibility that you'll experience with them and, therefore, your future financial security is not jeopardised by your relationship with them. In fact, they will look after your each and every need. Your sexual and emotional connections need work, however.

There's a powerful sexual connection with your Capricorn partner if they are born between the 2nd and the 10th of January. The planet of love, Venus, is clearly seen both in their personalities and their actions, even though they are generally ruled by Saturn. This will be a great love affair and also has the hallmarks of a permanent relationship that will satisfy the two of you.

VIRGO + AQUARIUS
Earth + Air = Dust

A relationship with Aquarius is one of those mysterious combinations that can either work or be a disaster, depending on how prepared the two of you are to work at it. Both of you are intellectually curious types. You'll have plenty to talk about and, even if you don't always agree, you'll still appreciate each other's viewpoints and have enough mutual respect to allow each other freedom in this respect.

Aquarius is a stubborn intellectual sign, however, and if you have any thoughts of changing their viewpoints over time, you're probably mistaken. They are staunch believers in political and cultural change and are considered the revolutionary individuals of the zodiac.

You are an earth sign and like things, to some extent, to stay fairly secure and grounded. Your Aquarian partner will want to shake things up, move things forward, turn things inside out and upside down. This could spin your head around, especially if it's done as forcefully and rapidly as the Aquarian sometimes works.

Expect the unexpected in a relationship with Aquarius. Sudden and explosive Uranus, their ruling planet, doesn't take any prisoners. You might think you have things under control and can deal with what's happening in the Aquarian world, but all of a sudden, unexpectedly the bomb will drop and completely and radically alter your life forever.

Work, service and professional interactions are strongly defined in the Virgo–Aquarius relationship. There is an element of Aquarius that mirrors your own desire to serve and perfect your work. Aquarius is more than happy to provide you with the support you need in your professional aspirations. In this sense, there's a good vibe between you.

The idealistic connection between you is karmic. The two of you can work together to create not only a good relationship for yourselves but also the world at large. You both aspire to higher, bigger and better things, not just for yourselves but for others as well, and this is in part due to the humanitarian instincts of your Aquarian partner.

VIRGO

You need to accommodate the rather wild and progressive sexual attitudes of Aquarius. They want you to let go, explore and revise your attitudes sexually. They want you to do it quickly, now; no, yesterday! So speed and change are the dominant aspects of your sexual, and to a large extent your emotional, interplay with them.

The best match with an Aquarian is with those born between the 31st of January and the 8th of February. The intellectual and communicative aspects of their personality mirror yours well and so you both have similar interests that will propel your relationship forward.

With Aquarians born between the 9th and the 19th of February, there's also a reasonably good compatibility and, if sexual expression is something you're looking for, then these people will fully satisfy you. For some reason, you won't be quite as intimidated in the bedroom with them and this therefore gives you the opportunity to explore your own sexuality freely.

With individuals born between the 21st and 30th of January, you need to be prepared for some challenges in the relationship. Initially, you may need to keep yourself at a distance until you understand them more. Professionally, you'll work well together and, as friends rather than lovers, this can be a good match.

VIRGO + PISCES
Earth + Water = Mud

If you're trying to analyse and understand your Piscean partner purely through intellectual means, forget it! You won't get very far. The Piscean personality is a complex maze that requires more than mental and deductive ability. You need heart to connect with a Piscean. They have profoundly developed spiritual and intuitive abilities. They operate on a wholly different level to most of the other star signs, so you need to enter this relationship with openness and humility.

The Piscean mind intrigues you but it also frustrates you, Virgo. You can't quite grasp where they're coming from and their dreaminess, their lack of practical direction, concerns you inasmuch as you like to have a clear idea of where your life is proceeding.

Pisces is the opposite sign to Virgo and, as they say, opposites do attract. The fact that you are so different could, in a strange way, be the reason that this relationship can work, and work well, if you're prepared to absorb some of the better qualities of each other and drop your preconceptions. Pisces is probably more able to do this than you are, so this relationship may indicate a greater challenge for Virgo than Pisces.

Both of you are born under the mutable component of the zodiac signs, which means you are highly changeable and indeed moody by nature.

VIRGO

When you encounter the Piscean mood, just allow them to work it through for themselves. With your critical and analytical mind, pointing out their flaws and how they can best improve themselves will only wound them and cause them to retreat into their shell.

You have a great chance of love and marriage with Pisceans born between the 20th and the 28th or 29th of February. These individuals have a more grounded approach than the typical Piscean and so it's likely you'll identify with this aspect of their personalities. I see a fulfilling relationship with them and you'll feel good about the fact that they're more open to listening to what you have to say about them.

Getting involved with a Pisces born between the 1st and the 10th of March is also an excellent combination. They are sensitive and loving individuals who'll provide you with the affection and mental stimulation you need. They also support you in anything you choose to do in life and I suspect that support will be mutual.

There's some great karma in store for you with Pisces born between the 11th and the 20th of March. The two of you are great communicators and can pool your resources to achieve something wonderful together. They're not particularly open to the way you criticise them but if you're able to develop your skills at diplomacy, they'll be more than willing to change their ways, improve themselves and in turn make this a much better relationship. If you are too swift in your criticisms, they may retaliate with fierce vengeance. Don't go there.

VIRGO

2010:
The Year Ahead

The future belongs to those who believe in the beauty of their dreams.

—Eleanor Roosevelt

Romance and friendship

You should consider yourself lucky this coming year, Virgo. The planets in 2010 are poised to provide you with an immense amount of joy and entertainment. You are serious about having fun and this is great because you may have been overly serious for way too long and now deserve a break. And the planets will give you that. Romance, friendship and other social pleasures highlight 2010.

You will feel alive, much younger and relieved of the burden of many of your past outdated relationships. This is certainly a new cycle and one you should look forward to with an open heart. Due to the transit of the Sun in your creative zone in January you will experience an upswing in your imagination. If previously you had postponed doing handicrafts, artistic hobbies or other pastimes near and dear to your heart, this is an excellent time to get cracking and explore your inner creative self again.

On the 18th of January Jupiter moves into your significant relationship zone, which dominates your most important personal relationships. An optimistic approach to love can be expected and you will also find others more open and demonstrative in their affection towards you. Married couples will feel as if it's time to renew their vows and, if you

VIRGO

aren't yet in a committed relationship, it's likely someone will come along and sweep you off your feet. For those of you in existing relationships, this is a time when the bonds of love can get stronger, and long-term commitments, including marriage, can be made.

You're idealistic about relationships this year and that is due to Neptune in close proximity to Jupiter as the year commences. You will want the best for yourself and expect your friends and lovers also to express their best to you. You want to display your love and ask others to reciprocate. Mostly you are the one that serves others' needs, but this year it's time for you to be pampered and waited upon. Don't feel guilty about this; you deserve the best, so go for it, Virgo!

In February you are emotional—perhaps a little too much. Don't wear your heart on your sleeve and don't let feelings dominate your decisions when it comes to love. You may also be moody, having a tendency to take out your frustrations on the ones you care about most.

You can expect a boost in your magnetic appeal with ample opportunities to attract potential friends or lovers. Particularly after the 11th, you're openhearted and ready, willing and able to involve yourself in a new love affair. This could present problems for you if you're already in a committed relationship because your wandering eye may get you into a spot of bother! Keep everything above board and don't get carried away in the emotion of the moment, especially if you're with a group of friends who are urging you to do things you wouldn't otherwise normally do.

March will usher in an important phase in your life and the more intimate aspects of your relationships will occupy much of your attention. You'll be seeking increased harmony and satisfaction through your marriage or will be trying to deepen your relationship with your significant other to take it to the next level. Much of your focus will be on money and how your shared resources will impact upon your personal affairs. However, try not to let these issues dominate the emotional and spiritual components of your love life.

You may start to see problems that aren't there, worrying about a situation that may never even come about. As with all relationships, honesty is the best policy, so talk about how you feel and, if you have any reservations, put your cards on the table and invite your partner to do the same. This transparent interaction will assist you in improving your relationship immensely.

Too many people demand too much of your attention and it would serve you well to prioritise your social engagements so that you don't run yourself into the ground. I can see your popularity growing to an ever-increasing level, but are you able to manage it? Your ego may get the better of you if you have the attention of several people. Always maintain humility. You don't want to run the risk of losing vital romantic opportunities.

VIRGO

You're on the go in April, and with the Moon and Venus triggering your itchy feet, travel is definitely on the cards. Mercury also stimulates your interest in foreign places or at least a change of pace. A shopping trip interstate, just taking it easy with friends for a weekend away, and generally taking a deep breath and time out from a hectic schedule will be a welcome relief for you. Believe it or not this could even involve a holiday romance that is totally unexpected. However, you may be disappointed when you can't take it any further and must simply enjoy the moment for what it is, without asking for too much more from it.

Enemies may be lurking in the shadows and you are unaware of this in May. Keep your wits about you and don't assume that everyone is your friend. You may not be the sort of person who pays much attention to gossip or hearsay and will write off what you hear on the grapevine as useless information. But there may be some damaging facts that come to light and you need to investigate the source more thoroughly before drawing your conclusions. Due to your popularity it's hardly surprising that there may be some people who are jealous of it and would love to cut you down for being a tall poppy. Soon enough you'll learn who these people are and you'll be better off without them.

As you reach the midpoint of 2010 several new opportunities in friendship and love make themselves clearly apparent. Venus and the karmic planets indicate an opportunity to reconnect with someone from your past or to befriend someone who has such common interests as yourself that it's hard to believe they are in fact strangers. Both of you will marvel at how closely knit your feelings are at such an early stage in the friendship. Your minds will think alike and your philosophical views may also be intertwined. This could be the start of a significant relationship.

Your idealism could cause you to seek pleasure and people who appear to be more than what they are during the months of July and August. Keep a level head and a good piece of advice for you at this stage of the year is to take some time out and reappraise who you are, what you want and whether or not the friends and lovers you associate with are fulfilling all of your needs. Naturally, none of us can be 100 per cent content with others, which is why this phase of the year beckons you to consider your own inner happiness as a focal point. By not relying wholly and solely on what others give you, you have a better chance of finding happiness.

Be careful of obsessive characters throughout September. You will open your heart to someone only to find that they are impossible to get rid of. There are some valuable lessons for you in the realm of romance at this time, but those lessons may cost you time and emotional happiness. Listen to your friends when they advise you of the ulterior motives of someone you are associating with. Ladies, if you are flattered by a younger man who is a smooth talker, you're likely to get your fingers burnt. Use your discretion, which may be difficult if you've had one too many drinks at a cocktail party. Exercise caution and good judgement to spare you some heartache.

The flames of your passion rage in October and hopefully you have someone who is in sync with you. You will feel the need to share this primal instinct with another like mind (or rather, like body!) because lust and pleasure will be dominating influences on you at this time. You can also be creatively passionate throughout November and December and, as the year comes to an end, it's likely you'll sense a great deal of satisfaction from what will be a year of fun, interesting new contacts and personal insights into love and romance.

As the year concludes, throughout November and December, try not to let the impulsive urges of Mars and the Sun distract your domestic happiness. Don't share your personal affairs with your relatives. By remaining tight-lipped about these issues you will avoid problems. Your family doesn't need to know everything about what is going on in your life.

Work and money

The year 2010 is one when you must reappraise your approach to money and finance. You may be like a dog with a bone, trying to work through financial issues, especially if you've overspent in the past and are now not earning quite enough to cover the bills. You have to look at this cycle as being one of creative financial management, otherwise you are likely to become disheartened by the situation, wondering when you'll turn the corner economically.

There are powerful forces in the area of your horoscope relating to speculation, particularly as the year commences. I ask you to hold back, even if you feel that you have a chance of making a lot of money in some daring course of action, and to wait rather than proceeding on a knee jerk reaction. You may believe there is a shortcut to financial success available to you, but this rarely happens and, along with hard work, a smarter attitude in your professional and financial affairs will be necessary for you to reach your goals in 2010.

There is some good news for you in February when Jupiter transits out of your zone of debt and into the public relations sector of your horoscope. This is excellent inasmuch as your entire focus no longer needs to be on your bills. In fact, there may be opportunities presenting themselves to you by way of negotiation that can indeed help you fast track your way into the black. Some new association can open exciting new doors professionally, which will result in a better salary for you.

In March and April business opportunities are accentuated by the movement of Venus and the Sun and shows you're popular with clients and able to secure the loyalty of your patrons to boost your earnings. Be careful, however, Virgo; you may be tempted to commit yourself to more expenses at a time when you are only just getting back on your feet.

VIRGO

This would be a grave error. Consolidate, I say, and build up your bank balance so that you can feel secure not just for a month or two but well into the future.

Luck is on your side throughout May and June when Venus transits the upper part of your horoscope, indicating a promotion and more cash in your pocket. This may not be something you have to work too hard for, either, because Venus is notorious for bringing luck through social contacts and your sheer popularity. There are, however, competitors ready to topple you and you must be a step ahead of them to solidify your position. You will be popular with your employers, who will help you with good advice.

You could be in two minds about your work in July and this is due to the additional responsibilities with which you are burdened. There's no point going backwards, Virgo. Meet your tasks head on, even if they are a little difficult to deal with for the time being. There are some Virgos who will opt to take the easy way out: rather than shouldering too much professional responsibility they will prefer to take a pay cut and enjoy more leisure time. There's nothing wrong with that, but it shouldn't happen at the expense of developing your abilities, technical skills and personal esteem. The result of cutting corners is that you'll only end up frustrated and in a dead-end. Balance the pros and cons carefully before committing yourself to a path of action.

Frustrations will be noted in August when Mars and Saturn hammer your financial zone. This may not relate so much to your inability to handle money as having differences of opinion with others to whom you are answerable financially. This may relate to family members, employers or other co-workers who have a different view on how money should be spent or saved. Listen to their viewpoint rather than reacting too strongly. There may be wisdom to be gained through such restraint and at the same time you won't damage your relationship with them by shooting them down in flames before they've had their say.

Contractual arrangements need to be carefully assessed in September and October. Because your habit by this time of the year will be to save money, it's likely you'll believe you are in a position to negotiate some complex fine print in a document. In fact, the better option will be to pay someone—a professional, a lawyer, perhaps—who can do the job far more quickly than you and spare you the embarrassment—or worse still, the cost—to come out of incorrectly signing something.

With Mars moving through your zone of real estate and property in November and December, it could be the perfect opportunity for you to consider ways to invest and make money through this avenue. As the year concludes, with Jupiter still in your zone of public relations, you're in a perfect position to strike up deals in all different areas of your life that are definitely to your own advantage.

Karma, luck and meditation

The year 2010 is an extremely lucky year for you because Jupiter will be directly influencing your Sun sign in a powerful way, bringing new and exciting people into your life, fresh business opportunities and generally a more prosperous time ahead.

Saturn, the tester, will challenge you financially but you mustn't let this deter you from thinking positively about the great opportunities Jupiter will bless you with. By all means tighten your belt but I believe firmly that jointly, these planets will ultimately shower you with extraordinary success, especially in the middle part of the year. Increased income through a better position, perhaps a promotion, or even a new job are possible.

By far the most important month for you romantically, and to a large extent karmically, is March. At this time the radiant Sun and Jupiter combine with loving Venus in your marital sector. This is an excellent omen for happiness in all areas of your relationships but particularly in your most intimate affairs. Engagements, marriage and other festive occasions are likely to occur—either your own or those of friends and family.

The other lucky months of the year for your activities are May and June when Venus pushes your professional prowess to an all-time high. Your popularity will be extraordinarily strong but you mustn't let the negative influences of other people deter you from your goals. With popularity comes enemies and, as I mentioned earlier, this is the time for you to rise above pettiness and to enjoy your success without letting others tear you down.

Finances are lucky in June and July when Venus moves through your profit sector. Unknown to most people, even to some astrologers, Venus in the twelfth zone of your horoscope in July makes you luxurious and capable of enjoying the money you've earned by lavishing gifts and other services on yourself. You deserve to have a good time, so see this as part of your karmic payback for good work and noble actions performed.

This lucky period continues throughout the year and is supported by the influence of Jupiter till December. Enjoy 2010 to the fullest!

… VIRGO

2010:
Month By Month Predictions

JANUARY

*I cannot give you the formula for success,
but I can give you the formula for failure, which is:
Try to please everybody.*

—Herbert Bayard Swope

Highlights of the month

Between the 1st and the 4th, your outgoing personality will win you many friends and possibly even an opportunity for real romance. Your personality will be much more bubbly than usual and this will attract others, even people you normally wouldn't expect to be drawn to you. Your mind will be keen to explore new avenues of personal relationships and, if you're currently involved with someone, this will be a time when you can thoroughly enjoy each other's company.

Between the 5th and the 7th, you mustn't let your moods interfere with the smooth functioning of your relationships. For some reason or other, possibly even unknown to you, you'll be feeling

VIRGO

down and unable to relate to your friends and family in your usual manner. Rest assured that this cycle will pass fairly quickly, so don't get too hung up on it. If need be, spend some time alone until the dust settles.

Your desire to further your educational qualifications could be triggered by discussions you have with a close friend around the 10th. This is a new cycle of mental and spiritual development that will also encompass a deeper understanding of human relationships generally.

After the 15th, your mind will be primarily concerned with your health and also the way in which others perceive you. You could be feeling self-conscious that you've put on a few extra kilos and naturally this will be bothering you in terms of your chances in attracting suitable partners or genuine friends overall. Apart from the impact this has on your social life, it's best to focus on the health benefits and just how great you can feel by committing yourself to a long-term strategy of physical exercise and changed diet.

From the 24th to the 27th, you'll be feeling sexually creative and will want to share some of your newfound knowledge with your spouse or lover. With Uranus still transiting your zone of marriage, it's quite likely you'll be developing a more progressive approach to your relationships, and matters of intimacy can't be excluded from this scenario. If you're with someone who is a little more traditional in the way they approach such matters, it would benefit you not to move too quickly because you're likely to scare them away. A slower, steadier approach to the exploration of your sexuality is necessary.

Between the 26th and the 30th, Mercury aligns well with your Sun sign and, being your ruling planet, promises to give you the edge in communications. Any important discussions that need to take place during this cycle will work to your benefit. Correspondence, communications by phone or Internet and e-mail will also provide you with some great social benefits. Put together those invitations for a function or get-together while you are riding the high of your mental creativity.

Romance and friendship

A brilliant idea to overhaul your family relationships is realised between the 6th and the 8th. This is a great time to pool together all of your family's resources and think carefully of ways in which you can integrate the different characters at home into one cohesive whole. Perhaps this is what your family's been waiting for—a hero to give them direction. You'll note that they will respond with enthusiasm, much to your surprise.

You'll have way too many options in terms of your relationships by the 13th. Choices, more choices and even more choices are likely to befall you during this period of the month. Let the passion within you help you make the right decision.

Also around the 13th, if you're trying to help someone through a dilemma, don't make yourself

VIRGO

an enemy. Listen more than you talk and try not to force them into a pathway which is against their nature. You'll be far more effective when listening rather than doing the talking.

The new Moon after the 16th is perfect for commencing a new relationship or friendship. You could meet someone who sweeps you off your feet.

Between the 18th and the 20th, love or rather lust seems to be the predominating influence in your life. Enjoy it fully and don't ask questions. Life is bringing you some pleasure for a good reason.

Friendships between the 23rd and the 28th are exciting and a little bit scary as well. You'll be asked to step out of the square and do something extraordinary. Why not?

On the 30th, don't allow your impulses to create troubles for you. What you hear should be kept as a secret and not passed on. No one likes a gossip but you may find yourself inadvertently revealing things you shouldn't.

Work and money

Between the 3rd and the 5th, you don't necessarily have to be sombre about money to make inroads and improve your financial worth. Keep your spirits light. The Moon and Saturn will cause you to feel a little down in the dumps because you haven't achieved your goal quickly enough.

You're idealistic about work between the 8th and the 13th. When Venus and Neptune conjoin, it means your passion and ideals will come together. You'll hit upon the right balance of effort and joy to make your work pleasurable.

For some Virgo-born individuals, the period of the 14th to the 16th is important in offering new work opportunities, either on the current job or at a new location. Applications for a new position are likely to be met with success.

The period of the 18th to the 22nd could see a great deal of confusion emerging in your workplace. An employer or co-worker may be ill or unavailable to do the job through personal circumstances and you'll be left to pick up the pieces.

From the 23rd, you'll have a dynamic uplift in your energy, which allows you to achieve your deadlines ahead of time. This promises to give you some spare time up your sleeve.

Destiny dates

Positive: 1, 2, 3, 4, 6, 8, 9, 10, 11, 12, 13, 16, 23, 24, 25, 26, 27, 28, 29

Negative: 6, 21, 22

Mixed: 5, 7, 14, 15, 18, 19, 20, 30

FEBRUARY

Highlights of the month

There's a good chance you'll have an opportunity to stand out from the crowd throughout February and, especially after the 2nd, you'll be in the limelight, the object of other people's attention and also their praise and blame. For most signs this wouldn't present too much of a problem, but being shy, as a Virgo is, it might present you with some discomfort. Nerves could get the better of you and you might spend days worrying, especially if you have to get up and talk at a social gathering.

After the 5th, when Mars imposes its energies on your zone of friendships, you'll have to fight for your friends and also for some of your personal ideals. There could be a conflict between them. You may realise that what you value is not really what some of your friends value, and vice versa. You may not have delved deeply enough into these subtle aspects of your life's purpose and your friends' philosophies. A showdown may occur and, if respect and honour for one another's differences don't prevail, this could be a difficult period, particularly up until the 15th.

After the 16th, Mercury provides you the opportunity to sort things out, to think things through clearly without your own personal bias impinging on the situation. This will call for clear and alert awareness with an objective view in mind. Mercury's position can also create obstacles in terms of enemies. You might not feel you've done anything wrong, but others don't seem to appreciate where you're coming from and could argue with you for the sake of proving you are wrong. They may not be able to do that, however, so you could create a few enemies in the process.

Venus comes to your rescue after the 20th, giving you a better, smoother run in your relationships. You have higher expectations for how these will go and can feel a greater harmony in your environment with your family and friends as well as others generally. Take the time to appreciate all the good things in your life and don't forget that an 'attitude of gratitude' has its own way of generating even more luck for you.

For Virgos who are moving house or planning big changes, the period of the 22nd to the 26th indicates a favourable transition. Communications will go well and you're not likely to experience too much of a delay in your plans. Your ideas are clear and bold but you may become a little bored with those you normally hang out with, who are not quite

VIRGO

as progressive in their thinking. This could cause you to look elsewhere, to increase and expand your circle of friends.

Romance and friendship

Between the 1st and the 3rd, you have an extra dose of communicative energy. Making calls and reconnecting with friends and lovers will be very fulfilling for you. Exchanging ideas, telephone numbers and engagement dates are all likely to occupy much of your time.

Between the 5th and the 8th, you mustn't embarrass yourself or those close to you by being too intense about your feelings. You may meet someone and will desperately want to take full advantage of the situation, only to find you're moving a little too quickly. Take things more slowly and enjoy the present moment rather than projecting into the future.

Sometime after the 11th, you'll realise you can't recreate those first moments of love in exactly the same way, simply because nothing stays the same. But you'll experience an elated spirit or a resurgence of love with your partner if you're in a relationship.

Trust your intuition between the 14th and the 17th. If you smell a rat, it's probably because there is one close to your vicinity. Spoken feelings and hidden motivations will be evident but don't forget it's sometimes hard to prove these things. It's probably best to wait a while if you're trying to catch out someone in a deceptive ploy.

After the 22nd, you have a lot more sexual magnetism. You could be attracted to all sorts of people—good and bad—and it's up to you to sift the chaff from the wheat.

Around the 28th, you'll find yourself in a situation where you can't quite express how you feel even though you can see the necessity of calling a spade a spade. You'll be tested with your patience and realise that the circumstances call for silence rather than outright honest opinion.

Work and money

You might confuse people on the 2nd because you realise you have to get a little more ruthless in the way you approach your work and your finances. Make it clear that it's nothing personal, just business.

Between the 7th and the 11th, you'll have to act as if you're the one in control, even if you're not. Just don't let your ego get in the road of doing the best job you can and treating people fairly.

Saturn moves into retrograde motion on the 14th, indicating a serious reappraisal of your finances. You need to put in place some new plans and strategies to organise your monetary situation. Tightening your belt is essential but this will be to your best advantage if you bite the bullet and take it seriously.

Between the 16th and the 19th is an excellent time to take stock of your financial position, but also balance that against the needs and status of your partner's assets. Growing your nest egg will be high on the agenda so assess your joint resources together.

Between the 27th and the 30th, you may have to decline a social offer because your bank balance doesn't allow it. Don't make apologies for this because you know what has to be done.

Destiny dates
Positive: 1, 3, 16, 17, 18, 19, 20, 22, 23, 24, 25, 26
Negative: 5, 6, 7, 8, 9, 10, 27, 28
Mixed: 2, 11, 14

MARCH

Highlights of the month

It's a hectic month for you romantically and socially with events happening at a breakneck speed, causing you to skim over some of your relationships between the 1st and the 6th. You'll be moving so rapidly from one person to another that they'll wonder whether or not you really have time for them, or even care. Be careful. Pay attention when others are talking to you, especially if you find yourself in a situation where it could be construed that you're more interested in hanging out with the 'names' rather than people who have something of value to offer you.

Around the 7th, some personal embarrassment or a minor confrontation could unsettle you for a few days. It's best to speak about how you feel rather than bottling up your feelings. You'll be averse to causing problems, but it may be unavoidable if someone in your group is picking on another who is less capable of defending themselves. You

VIRGO

may be forced to defend that person and thereby risk your relationship with the other.

Overall, between the 8th and the 15th, it would serve you well to consider the company you keep a little more carefully. If you're too busy to study the credentials of newcomers on the scene, there could be some later regrets. After the 17th, your ability to look at a situation, carefully assess it and give a friend some timely advice is likely.

Communications centre around your value systems again after the 18th. You need to sidestep arguments over money, over what you haven't got; or rather, who is contributing more than whom. If you look carefully at these discussions (or disagreements), you will clearly see that these problems are mostly nothing to do with money but deeper, long-standing emotional issues. Get to the crux of the dispute rather than distracting yourself with superficialities. Once you do this, your relationship will be back on course and in the right direction.

The period of the 20th till the 24th requires you to be flexible and adjust your behaviour and possibly even your thinking to others with whom you live or generally socialise. This could be pretty strenuous, as you may feel like a fish out of water, dressing, speaking or doing things in a manner you are unaccustomed to. But this may be essential to keep the peace.

Between the 29th and the 31st, you won't want to do much other than leisurely express yourself creatively by beautifying your home or sharing these ideas with a close friend. It's a nice finish to the month.

Romance and friendship

You feel a strong sense of freedom overtaking you this month and, with Venus and Uranus—the planet of independence and progressive thinking—dominating your horoscope, it's likely that anything will go.

Between the 1st and the 6th in particular, you'll be pushing your relationships to their limits. You'll be impatient for change and for a response that is in keeping with what your nature desires. If others aren't quick off the mark, you're likely to leave them behind.

Chance meetings are exciting and sexually activated after the 11th. Mars's movement in your zone of secrets could even indicate some sort of behind the scenes affair or relationship that resurfaces from the past. This simply requires an understanding of what you really want in your life before acting impulsively and wholly and solely from a carnal viewpoint.

What's good for the goose is good for the gander after the 14th. You'll find your spouse or partner is dishing out a little bit of what you've been giving them. A changeable mood, a nonchalant statement or, in fact, no response at all could leave you high and dry. You need to take as good as you give.

VIRGO

Your plans are thrown into a tailspin after the 17th and things could be left up in the air until the 23rd when you get clearer messages from the people who are involved. Don't rely on others to take control of planning when deep down you know you're the best one to take the lead.

Self-determination is much easier between the 27th and the 29th. You'll have the support of your friends and family members to implement a plan of action that has repercussions on your personal life.

Confusion is indicated on the 31st. Get clear directions before you leave home because you may find yourself taking much longer to get from A to B than you had at first planned.

Work and money

If you feel as though you're trapped, a prisoner of your own making, you have to accept the full responsibility for that. On the 2nd and the 3rd when the Moon activates your material instincts you might feel stifled by your job, in which you're not completely happy. You can't do anything about it because of commitments. Accept that the choices you make have repercussions and accept them with a smile. Things will get easier.

Between the 7th and the 15th you're lucky and may be the recipient of a legacy or small inheritance. Interest and accruals on your own savings seem to be larger than you expect as well. Generally, this is a good period to see an increase in your wealth.

Steady and constructive application to your duties will help you achieve your goals in the second half of the month. Between the 25th and the 30th, you can put forward a new strategy to your employer and expect a great response. Before you do, however, make sure you get a cut of the action.

Destiny dates

Positive: 25, 26, 27, 28, 29, 30
Negative: 1, 2, 3, 4, 5, 6, 17, 19, 20, 21, 22, 23, 24
Mixed: 7, 8, 9, 10, 11, 12, 13, 14, 15, 18, 31

Highlights of the month

With Venus moving through your ninth zone of foreign culture and travel, it's likely that a journey or holiday will take your fancy. Between the 2nd and the 8th, take that long-postponed vacation if you must, and go somewhere you've never been before. This can be an excellent time to reconnect with your lover and enjoy some foreign surroundings.

In the second half of the month, you could find yourself preoccupied with tedious communications that don't have anything to do with your own affairs. Being as service-orientated as you are, you'll feel duty-bound to help a friend or relative wade through some of their complex personal matters, which could bog you down for considerable time. The period of the 15th to the 18th will be particularly troublesome and requires you to make extra sacrifices for friends.

During April, you could feel rather uneasy about your relationships. There may be an underlying

2010: APRIL

sense of dissatisfaction or incompleteness and you may not be able to pinpoint exactly what is wrong. You'll feel cool and unemotional for the most part and you can attribute this to the planet Saturn retrogressing back into your Sun sign for a little while longer.

What this essentially means is that you will need to retrace your relationships; dig deep to see what it is or what was said or done that has subtly caused you to hold a grudge. These feelings may be operating on such an unconscious level that you may not be aware of your behavioural patterns stemming from some past hurt you feel has not been adequately resolved.

By the 22nd, you will feel a ray of sunshine entering your life and, with the Sun producing a favourable influence to the sign of Virgo, you will feel much easier about things and a lessening of the tension of Saturn. You'll be less inclined to argue a point and will value peace at any cost.

You mustn't knock back an opportunity to attend a lecture or study group around the 25th. This gathering will be a chance for you to meet someone new who will provide you with fresh insights, both into yourself and into your current and future relationships. There is a mentor on the horizon who could become a close friend. It's also likely this person could be either much older or younger than yourself. Don't let age be a barrier to developing this new relationship.

VIRGO

You can expect your social standing to jump in leaps and bounds from the 26th till the 30th. All manner of contact socially will work to your advantage, and it's likely that the introductions you make at this time will lead not only to great friendships but also business opportunities and some cold, hard cash as a bonus.

Romance and friendship

On the 1st and the 2nd, the Moon moving through the sign of Scorpio will bring out your more possessive and emotional personality traits. You're likely to be demanding with the result that others are not as likely to support you. Keep a hold on such feelings as envy and possessiveness.

Are you practising sport or some other outdoor pleasure? Competition is highlighted between the 5th and the 8th. You're likely to be determined to be the best at what you do. In matters of love, you're also as likely to be as competitive and will find yourself up against a contender in the field of romance.

On the 12th, you'll take some chances in love and will be attracted to the idea of conquest and the chase. It's great to be passionate but the downside of this is any residual scandal. Sex is going to be a very powerful means of expression for you till the 22nd.

Communications are difficult around the 18th when Mercury moves into its retrograde motion. It's likely mixed signals will produce delays in meetings, so it's important for you to get others to repeat instructions and intentions.

Between the 22nd and the 24th, any health concerns need to be traced back to your dietary and negative mental habits. These have an impact upon your physical wellbeing, but how aware are you of this? It's also a great time to get involved in service-related occupations and/or medical interests.

On the 30th, your spiritual aspirations are quite strong. You'll be keen to develop your reasoning and understanding of the meaning of your existence. You'll also want to share this with someone close to you. If you haven't been satisfied with your traditional religious or spiritual teachings, it may be time for an overhaul.

Work and money

After the 2nd, when Mercury enters your ninth zone of legal proceedings, you need to demand that everything be returned to you in writing. Get confirmation, not just verbally, because you may be stuck without proof at some future time.

Between the 7th and the 9th, power plays are evident. You need to learn the game of diplomacy and understand that others are prepared to crush you in a mad race to fulfil their selfish desires. You must be a step ahead of them.

When Saturn retrogrades out of your finance sector you may have some relief, however, from your financial constraints. This happens around the

VIRGO

10th and is a good omen for you, giving you a sense of release and a more relaxed attitude to your work generally.

Mercury goes retrograde on the 18th, so have all your paperwork ready and, if you don't, postpone the deal. You mustn't sign off on something you're not clear about.

Venus moving to your tenth zone of professional success on the 25th signals a wonderful new phase. You'll win popularity and are likely to gain the promotion you have had your heart on for some time. The bottom line is a better position and quite likely an increased cash flow coming your way.

Destiny dates

Positive: 3, 4, 5, 6, 7, 8, 10, 12, 25, 26, 27, 28, 29, 30
Negative: 1, 15, 16, 17, 18, 23, 24
Mixed: 2, 22

MAY

Highlights of the month

For those of you who are still feeling the impact of Saturn—that dull, rather monotonous energy that gives you the sense you're not getting anywhere in your relationships—it's likely that between the 1st and the 5th you'll do something dramatically out of character. You may want to throw all cares to the wind and push conventions to the limit.

Due to the position of Mars and the influence of Venus on your Sun sign, you may wish to explore the sensual part of your personality. To anaesthetise yourself from any pain or difficulties in your current relationship, you may do things that you could later regret. There's no harm in enjoying life after the 10th, even having a few drinks with friends and partying. However, if it's taken to the extreme, you'll not only embarrass yourself but can jeopardise your best relationships. Be more thoughtful of the consequences of your actions throughout the early part of the month.

VIRGO

Venus in your zone of friendship brings with it a whole new swag of social possibilities after the 19th. An array of parties, events and other social or group activities keep you busy during this phase of the year. Any type of gathering that you attend will go smoothly and be full of fun. Music and other forms of art seem to feature strongly. This could indicate a concert or possibly even a visit to an art gallery or fashion exhibition.

You'll feel out of sync with some of your peers between the 21st and the 23rd. If that's the case, stop fighting the flow of life and do something on your own. Is stepping out of the crowd all that big a deal? There may be issues of insecurity that you need to address. Your relationships will be on edge at this time.

If you've been single for a while, a blind date or an introduction to someone sometime around the 29th could prove to be nerve wracking. That may be so, but it's the perfect time to get out and show your best side. Extend your warmest energies out to the universe and you'll be pleasantly surprised at what that will bring back to you in return.

An important decision regarding your personal life may have to be made around the 30th. Don't procrastinate, and it's best not to rely too much on the opinions of other people who aren't familiar with your personal situation or needs.

Romance and friendship

You don't need to make too much of an effort to be

popular this month. On the 2nd, the Sun will create a wonderful aspect to your Sun sign, indicating that things seem to be falling together just nicely. Your expressive qualities will attract others and make them agreeable with you.

The period of the 4th to the 7th, however, shows that your manner may not be quite as cordial as it was in the first couple of days in the month. It's best to postpone any sort of important interview or situation in which you have to come across charmingly or graciously.

You can make your decisions firmly and decisively from the 12th. If you've been biting your tongue and need to clear the air, this is the time to do it. Mercury, moving in its direct motion, shows that you have the right words at the right time and can make a great impact on others. Even if you've got something to say that is not so pleasant, constructively putting forward your opinions will be greeted with appreciation.

Planning for trips should be done in concert with your friends this month, especially between the 14th and the 19th. You may want to delight others with some fantastic surprise, only to find that they are disappointed you didn't consult them in the first place. Perhaps you can give them a hint first and still keep something up your sleeve as the surprise?

Between the 28th and 30th, you could feel as though you're interfering with other people's affairs by pointing out the flaws in their behaviour but, unless you do it, it's going to bother you terribly. In fact, you may be asking yourself why you're with this or that person at all due to their immature behavioural responses.

Work and money

Take firm steps in your work around the 7th. Make a decision either way and stick to your guns. Be careful from whom you ask advice on the 12th. You may want the answers to some technical questions but could find yourself landed with too much 'geek' talk. You need a layperson who understands the technical side of things to bridge both worlds.

Between the 15th and the 20th, it's high time you took your ideas to the next level and showed the courage of your convictions. Now is the time to develop an independent pathway in business, if that's what you've dreamed of doing.

You're likely to have enough confidence now to put your best financial foot forward around the 22nd, so meet with your bank manager and ask for the loan or advance you'll need to get things rolling. This is the start of an exciting phase for those wanting to combine their creative ingenuity with business acumen.

After the 28th don't assume that the organisations you've invested your money with are all that impervious to market forces. Ask questions and, if you have any doubts, shift your investments to a more secure location.

Destiny dates
Positive: 2, 10, 14, 15, 16, 17, 18, 19, 20
Negative: 21, 23, 28
Mixed: 4, 5, 6, 7, 12, 22, 29, 30

Highlights of the month

You can learn a lot from older people, especially those who have been successful in their relationships, in marriage and love. Take the time to listen to their advice, especially if you've been banging your head against the wall, trying to work through some of your own emotional and personal issues. Someone you meet, perhaps an older person, has some valuable advice, but you must also apply it if you're to see yourself clear of any difficulties. Between the 1st and the 4th, make yourself available if an offer of help is extended to you.

Don't demand the loyalty of a friend after the 5th. This could only serve to scare them away and you'll be back to square one. A gentler and more persuasive approach will be necessary, and what do you feel is so hard about this, Virgo? Who says you're not charming enough to attract friends without demanding such a large slice of loyalty from them? It seems that this period of your life requires a little more self-confidence and self-love. That will definitely do the trick.

Communications with a friend or a lover on the 6th may require you to travel a considerable distance to prove your friendship to them. By doing so, you'll cement your relationship. Between the 9th and the 12th, you could be roped into some sort of joint social committee, in which you're reluctant to take part. Being as loyal as you are, you might find yourself biting off more than you can chew just to please your friends.

It's best to remain silent if your words aren't flowing smoothly between the 16th and the 18th. You might find yourself in a situation where, for the sake of sounding intelligent, you say the wrong thing and embarrass both yourself and others. Humility is the key word. Don't be afraid to admit that you don't know something; remember, people will respect you more for that.

Difficult planetary aspects continue to create some problems for your relationships between the 19th and the 20th. If your mind is not clear, it's best to refrain from making decisions or providing advice to others. And another thing: a strong suggestion is that you don't refer others to people or professionals. If the experience isn't good for your friends, they'll blame you for steering them in the wrong direction. This could cause bad blood when all you intended was to help them. 'The road to hell,' as they say, 'is paved with good intentions.'

VIRGO

The 29th and 30th are great days due to Mercury and its influence on your social affairs. Clear thinking and good company blend to produce a lovely climax to the month.

Romance and friendship

Family members and other close relatives will disagree with your viewpoint around the 4th, even though you're right. These individuals are living in the past and have no way of adapting to the current trends. But have the courage to stick to your own principles even when others don't accept your ways.

On the 6th and the 10th, you're highly strung. You could suffer nervous disorders or ailments associated with emotional stress. Talking with others may not help, so dig deeply into your own nature to find that space of equilibrium. What you find could be revealing on a spiritual level, especially when the Moon transits your ninth zone of spirituality between the 9th and the 11th.

You have to deal with divided loyalties and this will bring up a conflict of interest sometime after the 15th. You need to work behind the scenes and carefully prioritise who means what to you. Some of your friends are no longer friends because you've continued to superimpose some kind of outmoded value onto them. There now needs to be greater sharing between you to bring you back on course.

A ray of sunshine after the 21st brings relief in your close-knit circle of friends. This is due to the

Sun activating your zone of friendships and lifelong desires. What's more, it could be a healing period for you and close members of your family, particularly with your siblings or stepbrothers and sisters if you have them.

Between the 24th and 26th, you may suddenly discover something you'd forgotten and this will now be of value to you. Rather than it being a means of gaining some extra cash, the sentimental value will be far more important. On top of this, the nostalgia associated with this object will have you recollecting many old memories and friends from the past.

Work and money

Some born under Virgo may have been biding their time, waiting for the appropriate moment to pounce and prove that they have the energy and the dynamic drive to achieve what they want this year. For you, the 7th to the 9th is the likely time when Mars activates these drives and your physical energy will be much, much stronger.

Schedule meetings with employers and any other powerful individuals between the 10th and the 15th. You'll feel extra confident at the results you'll get. Because you'll be attentive to the details, it's also likely you'll be well prepared and rewarded for being so.

Virgos working in transport, travel, or jobs using machinery and heavy equipment, must exercise caution around the 18th. Mars tends to bring with

VIRGO

it the tendency to mishap, have accidents and incur other slight injuries. Even if you're in the home cooking, stop watching the news while you're cutting the onions or carrots. You're likely to injure yourself.

The 13th, 14th, 21st and 26th are important dates that promise a good cash turnover for Virgo. Call in any outstanding debts if you need to because you'll be able to do it in a way that doesn't offend those who are in the red to you.

The lunar eclipse of the 26th is particularly potent and relates to business transactions with young people or children.

Destiny dates

Positive: 1, 2, 3, 13, 14, 21, 24, 25, 26, 29, 30
Negative: 5, 6, 16, 17, 18, 19, 20
Mixed: 4, 7, 8, 9, 10, 11 12, 15

JULY

Highlights of the month

Why procrastinate any longer, Virgo? Between the 1st and the 6th, if you've been postponing making some important decisions about your relationships, it's best to get them over and done with now, as unpleasant as it may be. Especially around the 4th, you'll be particularly assertive about your ideas and what you want in life. You won't take no for an answer if you've been getting the raw end of the deal.

Please try to avoid gossip and hearsay between the 13th and the 18th. You'll hear secrets, innuendos and other malicious rumours, which you mustn't buy into. Apart from the social implications of this, it could also draw your mind to entertainment associated with conspiracy theories, politics and unexplained mysteries. This could be a link that draws you closer to a friend or group of people who are developing similar interests.

Delving into your past will be very important and, speaking of secrets, if there are aspects of your

VIRGO

past upbringing that have haunted you, then this is the time to get everything out into the open. Transparent discussions with your family will help bring these matters to light. If, for example, you suspect you were adopted or there are skeletons in the closet regarding potential relatives whom you've never met, look into these matters and clear the air. You'll be able to move forward with a clear conscience and then not have to look backwards again.

The impression you make after the 21st will be significant. New romantic alliances will be formed and these will be fulfilling, to say the least. Due to the strong connection of the Moon and Neptune, your ideals will be running very high. Your expectations, fantasies and even your sexual desires will seem to overtake you. Try to see others clearly rather than creating a web of delusions for yourself.

This is the time of the year to give yourself that special makeover, cosmetic surgery or at least a new hairstyle and colour. Venus will tell you that it's okay to splurge on yourself and make yourself look a million bucks, irrespective of the cost. This may cause some disputes when it comes to budgeting on the home front, but you're worth it!

On the 30th, the Sun moves to the spiritual and quiet area of your horoscope, which means you have an opportunity to reconnect with those subtle forces of nature, the deeper motivations of your life, so that you can get some real answers. Put up your 'do not disturb' sign and spend quiet time in reflection as the month of July draws to a close.

Romance and friendship

It may seem a strange thing to do, but creating a plan for your relationship is not a bad idea. Between the 1st and the 9th, you should spend time together mapping out the direction of your life and what it is you would like to achieve together. In doing so, you may discover a few differences as well. But this is all part of clarifying the common thread in your relationship, which will no doubt be very useful to you.

Cupid is hanging around your neighbourhood in the form of Venus moving through your Sun sign this month. You'll feel one, two, or maybe even more arrows shooting in your direction. Don't disregard them because this is truly a remarkable phase for generating interest and response from prospective partners.

The 10th to the 14th is a wonderful interval to develop your love of harmony, beauty, art and other social graces. It's also crucial you don't overlook etiquette as part of your educational life training just now. This will go a long way to furthering your 'aptitude', romantically speaking.

Good manners, dressing well for the occasion, and responding in the appropriate manner at the right time are all little things that go towards giving you the edge if you're looking for a lifelong partner.

You could increase your romantic quotient—and your partner's—by writing poetry, love notes and gesturing in new ways to entice and excite each

VIRGO

other from the 23rd to the 26th. Explore these different avenues to improve your love life.

Between the 25th and the 27th, you'll need to pay special attention to your family. If you've been overwhelmed with social engagements and the needs and demands of friends, spend some quality time with your relatives and your children. Right now, youngsters in particular may be demanding and excessively possessive of your time.

Work and money

Trying to conform this month may not be easy. On the 1st and the 2nd, you realise what has to be done, but don't have the support to push things through to the next level. If you're working with a constraining budget in some area of industry, you'll have to remember the old saying, 'necessity is the mother of invention', which is now quite applicable.

You see where you can be on the 8th, but are not accepting where you are. You can only do the best with what you've got, so don't beat yourself up. Plan more effectively.

Between the 10th and the 12th, you may inadvertently leak trade secrets or other sensitive information that was meant for only your ears and eyes. Rather than covering up the fact, you should make your error known to your co-workers or superiors now because it's likely this will come out in the wash sometime or other, anyway.

A deal or partnership you thought you'd had in the bag might have to wait a while longer after the

2010: JULY

26th. Accept that there are still facets of this deal or transaction that can be further refined to make it more advantageous for all parties concerned.

Destiny dates

Positive: 3, 4, 5, 6, 7, 9, 21, 23, 24, 30
Negative: 15, 16, 17, 18
Mixed: 1, 2, 8, 10, 11, 12, 13, 14, 25, 26, 27

AUGUST

Highlights of the month

This will be an excellent month to delegate excess work around the house to other family members. Why should you bear the full burden of everything that has to be done? You'll be able to create additional space, make time for yourself and also increase your vitality as a result. You'll have to put your foot down, though, because between the 2nd and the 6th, there could be some opposition to this. You'll be changing the status quo and others won't like it.

Inspiration will be on the top of your agenda. Between the 8th and the 10th, it will have a positive influence on your romantic affairs. In your relationships, you'll be able to express your feelings much more genuinely with the result that friends and lovers will reciprocate by being extremely affectionate in return. Explore your artistic and musical talents as well as your cultural awareness, which will be strongly highlighted.

It will be to your advantage not to overload yourself by taking on too much responsibility because you'll need time for your most personal one on one relationships. By the 15th, when Mercury creates havoc for you, you could find it hard to keep your mind on the job or whatever else is important in your life. There could be some difficulties in making decisions, and having too much on your plate will only confuse the issue.

With Mars and Saturn in close proximity, there could be many frustrations in your family generally. It's going to take considerable patience on your part to deal with your own feelings as well as those of your children, your partner and other relatives. You'll need to recharge your emotional batteries at some point and around the 17th or 18th would be a good time to do that.

Between the 20th and the 25th, new friendships that you strike up will have long-term repercussions for you. You could even meet someone who could be considered your soulmate. Don't become apathetic or negative about the quality of the people you're meeting because you could have second thoughts based on a wrong assumption. Around the 27th, you might find a relationship you had expected more from will unexpectedly appear indifferent or outright leave you high and dry. Things will not be as they had first appeared. You'll need more discussion as to what's needed to heal this relationship if you want it to go further.

Your social affairs move into top gear with loads of invitations arriving around the 29th. Some of your work commitments may get in the road of this but there's still ample opportunity to enjoy yourself during August.

Romance and friendship

On the 2nd your need for freedom and independence may conflict with the desire for love and some intimate companionship. You know you can't have your cake and eat it, too, so you'll just have to choose one or the other.

You're prepared to 'step out on a limb' between the 5th and the 7th and entertain those who are particularly off-beat or out of the ordinary. What would normally throw you off is now likely to arouse your curiosity and your appreciation as well.

Between the 10th and the 12th, look carefully for signals heralding someone's interest in you. Don't drink too much because you may miss some vital clues. Reach out to another person. Love will be reciprocal.

Changing your personal appearance is likely after the 15th. This will attract people to you. Unfortunately, their concerns, problems and ideals will be the main topic on the agenda, with you hardly being able to get a word in, edgewise. Your showing an interest in them will attract them to you, but that's not likely to be a two-way street.

The tendency for excess is noted and will

underpin many of your activities between the 20th and the 25th. Overdoing your eating, drinking and sexual pleasures may take its toll on you. Try to find a happy balance in your life because this will also help augment your health.

You feel quite relaxed and somewhat happy in your own company, so the urge to party with others between the 26th and the 28th is best postponed. The powerful energies of Mars, Saturn, Jupiter and Uranus could end up causing you more trouble than you expect. Disputes with family and friends are likely.

Weight gain is likely due to your excessive lifestyle. It's not a bad idea to rethink your gym membership and to scrutinise your calorie-counter book.

Work and money

You're frustrated by your work, your income and pretty much everything around you, due to Mars and Saturn settling between the Moon and Jupiter. This can play out in several different ways, but most likely it will make you lazy and lethargic. On the other hand, if people prod you at work, you're likely to retaliate and this could cause some rather nasty fall outs with people whom you normally get on well.

Assert your needs by all means after the 6th, but do it in a way that doesn't offend others. I have been saying to you all year: it's an excellent idea to put down your impressions in writing so there's a record of what's happened.

VIRGO

Professional issues are complicated around the 13th. Probably this has to do with your inability to listen to what's being said. Your impatience is a result of a build up of frustration and, the more you get angry, the less you listen, etcetera. It might help if you try to see the situation more objectively.

Your imagination is excellent between the 20th and the 25th. Use it in a constructive way. Mercury's retrogression gives you the opportunity to go back over old ground and to rectify errors.

Destiny dates

Positive: 8, 9, 17, 18, 29

Negative: 2, 3, 4, 13, 15

Mixed: 5, 6, 7, 10, 11, 12, 20, 21, 22, 23, 24, 25, 26, 27, 28

SEPTEMBER

Highlights of the month

This is a peak for most Virgos when the Sun and your ruling planet Mercury reassert their power by moving back into your Sun sign at this time. Particularly between the 3rd and the 8th, you'll feel enlivened by the power of these planets and also the emotional Moon. You'll have a greater level of intellectual energy and will want to develop your communication skills, both at home and in any new circumstances that present themselves.

Ideas are bubbling over and your enthusiasm will be contagious. Now that Mars and Saturn are separating from their dark and sombre influence on you, you should be able to share your thoughts and get the responses you want. The period between the 12th and the 16th should be a very bright and encouraging one for you.

After the 17th, if you are househunting and the going has previously been a little difficult, you'll notice a better calibre of house being made

VIRGO

available to you and also more amiable energies around the real estate agents and owners of properties that you may be looking at.

Your work and professional affairs receive a lift this month and this is due to the excellent placement of Mercury, which also governs your professional arena. You feel more secure and will be happy to receive some challenges from your employers, mainly because this will give you something to get your teeth into. This will not be a boring month at all. You'll be learning new things, sharing your concepts and plans with others, and receiving a fair degree of respect for your input.

Bureaucratic affairs mustn't be postponed, even if they are cumbersome and erode a lot of your time. You could find yourself going around and around in circles and will feel somewhat out of step with the culture of the organisations you have to deal with. You mustn't overlook important facts or figures because this could cost you additional time in submitting your paperwork. You need to get the dirty work out of the road to enjoy the remainder of the month.

Neptune continues to hover near the area of your romantic associations and also hints at the fact that someone you love, or a close friend at least, may be having some personal problems that require extra sensitivity on your part. After the 27th, don't be afraid to take the initiative and ask them what is wrong. They'll more than likely pour their heart out to you and you will definitely make a difference in speaking to them about these suppressed issues.

On the 29th and 30th, your romantic confidence is bolstered. If you've been in the emotional desert for a few weeks, some new friendships are likely to arise, which will also kick-start your confidence if it has been on the wane lately.

Romance and friendship

The Moon, Mercury and Venus are strong this month. Women will feature strongly in your life. A woman, perhaps an older one, will be of benefit to you between the 3rd and the 6th. If you become upset with some sort of problem, this person has a new angle that can help you out of your dilemma.

Between the 7th and the 10th, humour will be natural for you and your jokes will have others in fits of laughter. Your quick wit is going to be an asset, particularly when it comes to making friends, sharing your ideas, or even starting one of your crazy, harebrained schemes.

Between the 15th and the 17th you'll be on the go, hardly having time to eat your meals or really give anyone else the time of day. But you have to ask yourself, are you actually achieving anything? Perhaps you're skimming over some of your most important relationships, in the search for what?

Slow the pace a little and savour your friendships. Impulsiveness could lead to some regretful words around the 18th. Take special note of the cultural, religious or political background of the people you happen to be with.

Between the 20th and the 22nd an aspiration, a dream or expectation you have held for some time may come true. This could come in the form of your partner or spouse actually changing some habit and turning the corner in their attitudes. This will give you hope that your relationship can strengthen and have a greater future.

Between the 26th and the 30th you're extremely flirtatious, to say the least. Your warmth and lively personality will cause you to be the centre of attention. But be careful, you could also come on too strong for those who are somewhat more laidback.

Work and money

Don't get greedy this month. With the passionate Venus–Mars combination in your finance sector, greed could become very pronounced after the 2nd. There's no harm in aspiring to gain recognition and success, but don't let this override the quality of your work.

'Haste makes waste' after the 6th. You may be so busy driving yourself into the ground that you forget to count your change, check the bill at a restaurant, or remember where you placed your valuables. Check and recheck figures because you may have some difficulties with waiters, storekeepers and people who regularly serve you.

You're probably a little ahead of your time with

some of your ideas during this phase of the year. On the 18th and 19th, try to explain things in a simpler manner and, if you have technical abilities, remember that others aren't always as 'au fait' with the lingo as you are. Try to cater to the least common denominator as far as your listeners are concerned, particularly if you happen to be giving a talk, lecture or training session.

You're indeed shining this month due to the placement of the Sun in your sign of Virgo. You should see an increase in your popularity, your health should also improve, and your general fortunes, particularly in your working life, will be improving day by day. These great energies should reach a peak around the 28th.

Destiny dates

Positive: 3, 4, 5, 6, 7, 8, 9, 10, 12, 13, 14, 20, 21, 22, 26, 28, 29, 30

Negative: 6, 18, 19

Mixed: 2, 15, 16, 17, 27

Highlights of the month

This month is one of considerable financial responsibility. The Sun with Saturn in your zone of finance is challenged by the Moon between the 1st and the 10th. You can't afford to be emotional about finances and the way money is spent or saved. In other words, what I'm saying to you is that you have to be ruthless. You may try to make decisions with your heart, but this won't work.

It serves you well to develop your relationship with your employers—or people who supervise or work in close quarters with you—because sometime around the 15th, you may receive some rather unpleasant news. By relying on your professional allies, your mentors and those who have your best interests in mind, you can easily come to a solution.

On the other hand, if you try to go it alone and let your ego dominate the situation, you'll find yourself stuck. Put your pride aside and admit you

2010: OCTOBER

don't know everything and that there are others who can help you through difficult patches. By doing this, you'll clear the decks and be able to be more productive in the latter part of the month.

By the 20th, you will want to be out and about and Mercury will be creating many new opportunities; as well as the tendency to overindulge yourself. Try not to overdo it and, even if your intellectual curiosity gets the better of you, try to postpone important decisions until you're satisfied you have all the information required to make appropriate ones.

Communication is also important where it comes to passionately losing your self-control. There are ample opportunities to mix and romanticise with potential lovers during October, but not all of them will give you the fulfilment you are after. You have to be a step ahead of the game and start looking more deeply into other people's motivations. Your brain probably knows what's going on from the beginning, but your heart wants to believe there's more to it. Stop deluding yourself and play hard ball with the pretenders.

Your charitable instincts come to the fore after the 26th and you'll do something without thought of gain. Surrendering to a more compassionate side of your nature will yield some wonderful spiritual results for you. You may even want to get involved personally and take control of a type of charitable organisation or raffle that may be part of your office scenario. I suggest you give it your best shot,

VIRGO

because you'll not only make a difference in the world, but could even meet some new people with whom you will develop long-term relationships.

Romance and friendship

Are you afraid of being alone, Virgo? Many people, as they reach the middle part of their lives, believe they have a dilemma if they are still single. You might feel this is your problem, especially between the 2nd and the 7th. But, is it a dilemma? Putting up with less than the best for fear you may not have anyone at all is a mistake, and hopefully you'll be able to see that. Why not set your personal values much higher?

The 10th to the 14th is a rather difficult period with the Sun and Saturn indicating that additional family responsibilities are weighing you down. You'll find it difficult balancing your family needs against those of your own personal desires.

Between the 10th and the 15th, hold off before becoming too quickly involved with someone you meet. This is what I said earlier about settling for second best. You do deserve better, so reaffirm that fact.

You could be out of sync with your peers between the 13th and the 17th. In fact, your viewpoints could differ so strongly that you may fall out of favour with one or more of them. Sometimes it's best not to share your intentions with others. This could be one of those times where you need to keep your own cards close to your chest.

A past relationship, which previously has had loose ends, needs to be dealt with around the 20th. Circumstances could develop quite unexpectedly. Don't overreact when you get a call or hear news of this particular person and their goings-on. You need to drop the past; but if it's unavoidable, deal with it calmly and fairly.

The decision of a family member could get you all riled up. It may be a good time to step out of the scene and spend some time alone.

Work and money

To prove your worth you may have to do things that are not pleasant. This reminds me of an old saying, which goes something like, 'the good is not necessarily pleasant!' Some of your tasks will be tedious this month, especially between the 4th and the 10th. This can't help but happen due to the difficult combination of the Sun and Saturn.

Contracts are favourable for you this month, but only if you wait until after the 15th. In fact, a better set of planetary circumstances then appears when the Moon joins Jupiter in your zone of business contacts and partnerships.

Contracts are also likely to be a feature of your life around the 23rd. These issues are highlighted yet again due to the fact that the Sun enters your zone of contracts on the same day.

Personal power, social life and mixing with those in authority all come together between the

VIRGO

25th and the 28th. When the Sun conjoins Venus in your third zone of communication, some important discussions will take place with some good financial consequences.

Destiny dates

Positive: 23, 25, 26, 27, 28
Negative: 1, 2, 3, 4, 5, 6, 7, 8, 9
Mixed: 10, 11, 12, 13, 14, 15, 20

NOVEMBER

Highlights of the month

Between the 2nd and the 8th, the more you try, the less fulfilling your results will be. On the other hand, the more relaxed and passive you are, the more likely you will be to gain the support of your friends and co-workers. This sounds like it's back to front, doesn't it? This is a radical approach to achieving what you want in life. It is part of the spiritual law of the universe, and you should try it. You actually need less than what you're going after. This attitude will magically attract many new opportunities, money, and even friends and romantic partners, if that's what you're looking for.

Between the 10th and the 15th, you may be quietly concerned about how you are coming across to the world around you. There could be a vague dissatisfaction that you haven't yet achieved everything you want to achieve, so you must remember that 'Rome wasn't built in a day'. Try to exercise patience but more importantly remember to enjoy the journey of your life and not expect things to

VIRGO

happen overnight, otherwise you'll miss what's happening now and that is as beautiful as what you hope to achieve in the future. Remain philosophical this month and you'll be much happier.

Venus will tempt you once again into spending lavishly, especially on yourself. I say it's important to pamper yourself and reward yourself for hard work, but this could be one of those times where you can ill afford to spend too much. Perhaps you can look at reducing the cost of those items and still give yourself the treat you desire? But remember, the presence of Saturn will continue to try to teach you the lesson of frugality and self-restraint.

Problems could be encountered between the 18th and the 22nd, and debts, especially those of your own making, might become a greater problem than you expect. This is also shown by the very powerful combination of Jupiter and Uranus, both of which are in retrogression. You might believe that your gambling or excessive tendencies will pay off, but that's a short-sighted approach. Reflect a little more carefully on your financial affairs before going crazy with your spending.

After the 23rd, intimate and personal aspects of your life will take precedence. If you've had issues of trust bothering you—and this is likely due to the fact that Mars and also Saturn are having a joint influence over these areas of your life—you will want to put these matters to rest once and for all.

There is no point arguing a matter, even if you are right. Someone you encounter in your personal

2010: NOVEMBER

life will be as stubborn as a mule and won't listen to reason. Listen to their side of the story because this will make them feel you care about what's happening to them. Then make your move.

Between the 28th and 30th collaborate with neighbours so that borderline conflicts and silly long-standing disagreements can be resolved to everyone's satisfaction.

Romance and friendship

On the 1st, your mind is drawn inwardly and it's best for you to stay out of the limelight. Even if you see an opportunity to help others in your family, it's best to remain uninvolved. Let second and third parties deal with their own problems on the home front.

In the outside world, however, compassionate work, humanitarian aid and other forms of selfless service will be spotlighted throughout November. You'll tire of any remnants of a hedonistic lifestyle and want something more meaningful. You'll definitely have the opportunity to mix with those of high spiritual calibre. On the 5th your spiritual aspirations are highlighted and on the 6th you're likely to have important realisations about life.

A flash flood of emotional energies heading your way between the 7th and the 9th should also be a caution for you to lay low and not stick your nose into business that doesn't concern you. Just because you happen to be part of a family doesn't mean that you have to act as the mediator, judge, jury and executioner.

VIRGO

You're intense about your love life between the 10th and the 14th. You may want more out of your relationship but may not quite know how to go about eliciting the right response from your partner. In times such as these, it's not always about what you say so much as what you do, because any gestures and looks involved largely impact on what's happening.

Some straightforward discussions between the 21st and the 24th are necessary. Mercury and Mars give you keen insights and a deductive mind, which are useful for solving problems. This is an excellent time to bury the hatchet if you've been having disputes with others.

From the 24th to the 29th your social life is once again activated in a positive way. Someone may give you a gift for no other reason than as an act of appreciation for you being there for them in the past.

Work and money

Between the 1st and the 4th you mustn't rely on other people to do your work for you, especially if important documents have to be passed from one person to another. What happens if you don't have backups of your work, or the information is lost? This is precisely what may occur. Take full personal responsibility for these matters.

Seriously consider construction, renovation and other home or work improvements this month. The 7th, 8th and 9th are perfect days to get your hands dirty and finally clear the backlog of home work that has been bothering you.

Investment in housing, real estate and other speculative ventures is likely between the 9th and the 14th. However, get good advice before reaching into your pocket.

Educational endeavours should be pursued with a vengeance between the 19th and the 22nd. Whatever topic takes your interest—even if it doesn't seem related to your current line of work—will, at some point, be useful to you.

Between the 26th and the 29th the solution you're looking for to a problem is not exactly what you think it might be. Think laterally outside the square and, magically, the solution will appear.

Destiny dates

Positive: 28, 29, 30

Negative: 2, 3, 4, 7, 8, 9, 18, 19, 20

Mixed: 1, 5, 6, 10, 11, 12, 13, 14, 15, 21, 22, 23, 24

DECEMBER

Highlights of the month

December can be a fun month but you have to be prepared to let down your guard and stop holding onto the old baggage. There may still be issues surrounding your family, but it's best to put these aside for the moment because it's quite likely you won't be able to resolve them fully until the new year. Between the 1st and the 7th, make a commitment to yourself that you're going to forget all of the previous trivia and get down to having some real fun. Get ready for Christmas and simply do what you can to enjoy life to the fullest!

This could be an extraordinarily creative time of the year, a great way to complete 2010, so work on that side of your life as well.

And, speaking about creativity, you have to be open to what your partner or friend feels is creative in their universe. After the 10th, you'll be invited to try something new but could feel reluctant to do so. You may be embarrassed—self-conscious—about your inability to shine in that particular area. But that doesn't matter, does it? This is an opportunity to have fun; to show your partner or your friend or your spouse that you're prepared to support them in their creative endeavours as well.

Remember, it's not all about you, and even though as a Virgo you are one of the more evolved types when it comes to service, there may be something that sticks in your throat over this matter and it's simply up to you to let go of everything and try the untried.

For singles born under Virgo, the wonderful aspect between Venus and Jupiter is a great omen for an end of year romance. Make yourself available and be prepared to open your heart to strangers. However, don't judge too soon because Uranus indicates meetings with those who are completely out of your usual sphere of a perfect partner.

With the Sun entering your fifth zone of entertainment, creativity and competitiveness, you'll be enlivened over the Christmas period. It generates a tremendously positive influence on your Sun sign of Virgo. Get ready for a fun-filled, zestful and up-beat festive season!

You'll look back on 2010 as having been one of the better years of your life, with your creative spark bursting into flames of joy and great productivity. Between the 27th and the 30th, this should continue to be evident by means of a confident air about you, of a promise that things in 2011 will be even better.

VIRGO

Romance and friendship

You'll be able to move forward on the home front and this is likely around the 5th. You may, however, have to get someone else to do your dirty work, so to speak, and that's not a bad idea. It sounds horrible, but at least if someone has to get 'shot', it will be the 'messenger', not you.

You can reach for what you want in your love life and not settle for anything less than you dream of. On the 9th, keep your pen handy and don't be afraid to jot down the qualities—both mental and physical—you expect to find in your soulmate.

There's a lot of activity at home in December and you'll opt to have the Christmas dinner on your own turf. Make sure those you invite—if they include people who are not directly related to you—are well suited for compatibility. This will help avoid some of those Christmas dramas between conflicting characters. All in all, however, it seems like this may be an enjoyable and fun-filled Christmas.

Mercury's retrogression after the 10th continues through till the 30th. Many of your personal traits, both good and bad, will be highlighted. But because you're noted for your desire to improve yourself, this will enhance all your relationships and is going to act as an antidote to any problems at the Christmas dinner table.

The final important transits of 2010 include the Moon with Saturn and then Venus on the 29th and again on the 31st. This reflects the love, but

2010: DECEMBER

seriousness, associated with your friendships and relationships, and your continuing commitment to making your love life even better in 2011.

Work and money

You mustn't fight about money in December. Be generous and give, even if you feel as though there seems to be an imbalance in the equation of who's giving more than who. These matters could occupy your mind between the 1st and the 7th, but don't dwell too much on them.

Don't procrastinate on the 10th. Things could slide sideways and you'll be waiting a couple of weeks till you can get a clear answer. Push a little harder before that date to catch things in the bag.

The lunar eclipse on the 21st is significant. It may be timely for you to pull back from excessive work practices and try to divide your time between home and work by doing some of your preparatory groundwork at home, rather than spending inordinate amounts of time away from your family and loved ones.

Finally, remember one of the important themes for the year has been to keep things light and breezy and not to take money so seriously. Hopefully the wonderful aspect of Venus to Neptune will help you realise the value of work as being not just what you're going to earn from it financially.

Destiny dates
Positive: 1, 2, 3, 4, 5, 6, 7, 27, 28, 29, 30, 31
Negative: Nil
Mixed: 10, 21

VIRGO

2010:
Astronumerology

The future ain't what it used to be.

—Yogi Berra

The power behind your name

By adding the numbers of your name you can see which planet is ruling you. Each of the letters of the alphabet is assigned a number, which is listed below. These numbers are ruled by the planets. This is according to the ancient Chaldean system of numerology and is very different to the Pythagorean system to which many refer.

Each number is assigned a planet:

AIQJY	=	1	**Sun**
BKR	=	2	**Moon**
CGLS	=	3	**Jupiter**
DMT	=	4	**Uranus**
EHNX	=	5	**Mercury**
UVW	=	6	**Venus**
OZ	=	7	**Neptune**
FP	=	8	**Saturn**
—	=	9	**Mars**

Notice that the number 9 is not aligned with a letter because it is considered special. Once the numbers have been added you will see that a single planet rules your name and personal affairs. Many famous actors, writers and musicians change their names

VIRGO

to attract the energy of a luckier planet. You can experiment with the list and try new names or add the letters of your second name to see how that vibration suits you. It's a lot of fun!

Here is an example of how to find out the power of your name. If your name is John Smith, calculate the ruling planet by assigning each letter to a number in the table like this:

J O H N S M I T H
1 7 5 5 3 4 1 4 5

Now add the numbers like this:
$1 + 7 + 5 + 5 + 3 + 4 + 1 + 4 + 5 = 35$
Then add $3 + 5 = 8$

The ruling number of John Smith's name is 8, which is ruled by Saturn. Now study the name-number table to reveal the power of your name. The numbers 3 and 5 will also play a secondary role in John's character and destiny, so in this case you would also study the effects of Jupiter and Mercury.

Name-number table

Your name number	Ruling planet	Your name characteristics
1	**Sun**	Magnetic individual. Great energy and life force. Physically dynamic and sociable. Attracts good friends and individuals in powerful positions. Good government connections. Intelligent, impressive, flashy and victorious. A loyal number for relationships.
2	**Moon**	Soft, emotional nature. Changeable moods but psychic, intuitive senses. Imaginative nature and empathetic expression of feelings. Loves family, mother and home life. Night owl who probably needs more sleep. Success with the public and/or women.
3	**Jupiter**	Outgoing, optimistic number with lucky overtones. Attracts opportunities without trying. Good sense of timing. Religious or spiritual aspirations.

VIRGO

Your name number	Ruling planet	Your name characteristics
		Can investigate the meaning of life. Loves to travel and explore the world and people.
4	**Uranus**	Explosive character with many unusual aspects. Likes the untried and novel. Forward thinking, with many extraordinary friends. Gets fed up easily so needs plenty of invigorating experiences. Pioneering, technological and imaginative. Wilful and stubborn when wants to be. Unexpected events in life may be positive or negative.
5	**Mercury**	Quick-thinking mind with great powers of speech. Extremely vigorous life; always on the go and lives on nervous energy. Youthful attitude and never grows old. Looks younger than actual age. Young friends and humorous disposition. Loves reading and writing.
6	**Venus**	Delightful personality. Graceful and attractive character who cherishes friends

Your name number	Ruling planet	Your name characteristics
		and social life. Musical or artistic interests. Good for money making as well as abundant love affairs. Career in the public eye is possible. Loves family but is often overly concerned by friends.
7	**Neptune**	Intuitive, spiritual and self-sacrificing nature. Easily misled by those who need help. Loves to dream of life's possibilities. Has curative powers. Dreams are revealing and prophetic. Loves the water and will have many journeys in life. Spiritual aspirations dominate worldly desires.
8	**Saturn**	Hard-working, focused individual with slow but certain success. Incredible concentration and self-sacrifice for a goal.
		Money orientated but generous when trust is gained. Professional but may be a hard taskmaster. Demands highest standards and needs

VIRGO

to learn to enjoy life a little more.

9   **Mars**   Fantastic physical drive and ambition. Sports and outdoor activities are keys to wellbeing. Confrontational. Likes to work and play just as hard. Caring and protective of family, friends and territory. Individual tastes in life but is also self-absorbed. Needs to listen to others' advice to gain greater success.

Your 2010 planetary ruler

Astrology and numerology are very intimately connected. As already shown, each planet rules over a number between 1 and 9. Both your name *and* your birth date are ruled by planetary energies.

Add the numbers of your birth date and the year in question to find out which planet will control the coming year for you.

For example, if you were born on the 12th of November, add the numerals 1 and 2 (12, your day of birth) and 1 and 1 (11, your month of birth) to the year in question, in this case 2010 (the current year), like this:

$1 + 2 + 1 + 1 + 2 + 0 + 1 + 0 = 8$

2010: ASTRONUMEROLOGY

The planet ruling your individual karma for 2010 will be Saturn because this planet rules the number 8.

You can even take your ruling name-number as shown earlier and add it to the year in question to throw more light on your coming personal affairs, like this:

John Smith = 8

Year coming = 2010

$8 + 2 + 0 + 1 + 0 = 11$

$1 + 1 = 2$

Therefore, 2 is the ruling number of the combined name and date vibrations. Study the Moon's number 2 influence for 2010.

Outlines of the year number ruled by each planet are given below. Enjoy!

1 is the year of the Sun

Overview

The Sun is the brightest object in the heavens and rules number 1 and the sign of Leo. Because of this the coming year will bring you great success and popularity.

You'll be full of life and radiant vibrations and are more than ready to tackle your new nine-year cycle, which begins now. Any new projects you commence are likely to be successful.

Your health and vitality will be very strong and your stamina at its peak. Even if you happen to have

VIRGO

the odd problem with your health, your recuperative power will be strong.

You have tremendous magnetism this year so social popularity won't be a problem for you. I see many new friends and lovers coming into your life. Expect loads of invitations to parties and fun-filled outings. Just don't take your health for granted as you're likely to burn the candle at both ends.

With success coming your way, don't let it go to your head. You must maintain humility, which will make you even more popular in the coming year.

Love and pleasure

This is an important cycle for renewing your love and connections with your family, particularly if you have children. The Sun is connected with the sign of Leo and therefore brings an increase in musical and theatrical activities. Entertainment and other creative hobbies will be high on your agenda and bring you a great sense of satisfaction.

Work

You won't have to make too much of an effort to be successful this year because the brightness of the Sun will draw opportunities to you. Changes in work are likely and, if you have been concerned that opportunities are few and far between, 2010 will be different. You can expect some sort of promotion or an increase in income because your employers will take special note of your skills and service orientation.

Improving your luck

Leo is the ruler of number 1 and, therefore, if you're born under this star sign, 2010 will be particularly lucky. For others, July and August, the months of Leo, will bring good fortune. The 1st, 8th, 15th and 22nd hours of Sundays especially will give you a unique sort of luck in any sort of competition or activities generally. Keep your eye out for those born under Leo as they may be able to contribute something to your life and may even have a karmic connection to you. This is a particularly important year for your destiny.

Your lucky numbers in this coming cycle are 1, 10, 19 and 28.

2 is the year of the Moon

Overview

There's nothing more soothing than the cool light of the full Moon on a clear night. The Moon is emotional and receptive and controls your destiny in 2010. If you're able to use the positive energies of the Moon, it will be a great year in which you can realign and improve your relationships, particularly with family members.

Making a commitment to becoming a better person and bringing your emotions under control will also dominate your thinking. Try not to let your emotions get the better of you throughout the coming year because you may be drawn into the changeable nature of these lunar vibrations as well. If you fail to keep control of your emotional life you'll later regret some of your actions. You must blend careful thinking with feeling to arrive at the best results. Your luck throughout 2010 will certainly be determined by the state of your mind.

Because the Moon and the sign of Cancer rule the number 2 there is a certain amount of change to be expected this year. Keep your feelings steady and don't let your heart rule your head.

Love and pleasure

Your primary concern in 2010 will be your home and family life. You'll be finally keen to take on those renovations, or work on your garden. You may even think of buying a new home. You can at last carry out some of those plans and make your dreams come true. If you find yourself a little more temperamental than usual, do some extra meditation and spend time alone until you sort this out. You mustn't withhold your feelings from your partner as this will only create frustration.

Work

During 2010 your focus will be primarily on feelings and family; however, this doesn't mean you can't make great strides in your work as well. The Moon rules the general public and what you might find is that special opportunities and connections with the world at large present themselves to you. You could be working with large numbers of people.

If you're looking for a better work opportunity, try to focus your attention on women who can give you a hand. Use your intuition as it will be finely tuned this year. Work and career success depends upon your instincts.

Improving your luck

The sign of Cancer is your ruler this year and because the Moon rules Mondays, both this day of the week and the month of July are extremely lucky for you. The 1st, 8th, 15th and 22nd hours on Mondays will be very powerful. Pay special attention to the new and full Moon days throughout 2010.

The numbers 2, 11 and 29 are lucky for you.

3 is the year of Jupiter

Overview

The year 2010 will be a number 3 year for you and, because of this, Jupiter and Sagittarius will dominate your affairs. This is extremely lucky and shows you'll be motivated to broaden your horizons, gain more money and become extremely popular in your social circles. It looks like 2010 will be a fun-filled year with much excitement.

Jupiter and Sagittarius are generous to a fault and so, likewise, your open-handedness will mark the year. You'll be friendly and helpful to all of those around you.

Pisces is also under the rulership of the number 3 and this brings out your spiritual and compassionate nature. You'll become a much better person, reducing your negative karma by increasing your

VIRGO

self-awareness and spiritual feelings. You will want to share your luck with those you love.

Love and pleasure

Travel and seeking new adventures will be part and parcel of your romantic life this year. Travelling to distant lands and meeting unusual people will open your heart to fresh possibilities of romance.

You'll try novel and audacious things and will find yourself in a different circle of friends. Compromise will be important in making your existing relationships work. Talk about your feelings. If you are currently in a relationship you'll feel an upswing in your affection for your partner. This is a perfect opportunity to deepen your love for each other and take your relationship to a new level.

If you're not yet attached to someone, there's good news for you. Great opportunities lie in store and a spiritual or karmic connection may be experienced in 2010.

Work

Great fortune can be expected through your working life in the next twelve months. Your friends and work colleagues will want to help you achieve your goals. Even your employers will be amenable to your requests for extra money or a better position within the organisation.

If you want to start a new job or possibly begin an independent line of business, this is a great year to do it. Jupiter looks set to give you plenty of opportunities, success and a superior reputation.

Improving your luck

As long as you can keep a balanced view of things and not overdo anything, your luck will increase dramatically throughout 2010. The important thing is to remain grounded and not be too airy-fairy about your objectives. Be realistic about your talents and capabilities and don't brag about your skills or achievements. This will only invite envy from others.

Moderate your social life as well and don't drink or eat too much as this will slow your reflexes and weaken your chances for success.

You have plenty of spiritual insights this year so you should use them to their maximum. In the 1st, 8th, 15th and 24th hours of Thursdays you should use your intuition to enhance your luck, and the numbers 3, 12, 21 and 30 are also lucky for you. March and December are your lucky months but generally the whole year should go pretty smoothly for you.

4 is the year of Uranus

Overview

The electric and exciting planet of the zodiac, Uranus, and its sign of Aquarius, rule your affairs throughout 2010. Dramatic events will surprise and at the same time unnerve you in your professional and personal life. So be prepared!

VIRGO

You'll be able to achieve many things this year and your dreams are likely to come true, but you mustn't be distracted or scattered with your energies. You'll be breaking through your own self-limitations and this will present challenges from your family and friends. You'll want to be independent and develop your spiritual powers and nothing will stop you.

Try to maintain discipline and an orderly lifestyle so you can make the most of these special energies this year. If unexpected things do happen, it's not a bad idea to have an alternative plan so you don't lose momentum.

Love and pleasure

You want something radical, something different in your relationships this year. It's quite likely that your love life will be feeling a little less than exciting so you'll take some important steps to change that. If your partner is as progressive as you'll be this year, then your relationship is likely to improve and fulfil both of you.

In your social life you will meet some very unusual people, whom you'll feel are especially connected to you spiritually. You may want to ditch everything for the excitement and passion of a completely new relationship, but tread carefully as this may not work out exactly as you expect it to.

Work

Technology, computing and the Internet will play a larger role in your professional life this coming year.

You'll have to move ahead with the times and learn new skills if you want to achieve success.

A hectic schedule is likely, so make sure your diary is with you at all times. Try to be more efficient and don't waste time.

New friends and alliances at work will help you achieve even greater success in the coming period. Becoming a team player will be even more important in gaining satisfaction from your professional endeavours.

Improving your luck

Moving too quickly and impulsively will cause you problems on all fronts, so be a little more patient and think your decisions through more carefully. Social, romantic and professional opportunities will come to you but take a little time to investigate the ramifications of your actions.

The 1st, 8th, 15th and 20th hours of any Saturday are lucky, but love and luck are likely to cross your path when you least expect it. The numbers 4, 13, 22 and 31 are also lucky for you this year.

5 is the year of Mercury

Overview

The supreme planet of communication, Mercury, is your ruling planet throughout 2010. The number 5, which is connected to Mercury, will confer upon you success through your intellectual abilities.

Any form of writing or speaking will be improved

VIRGO

and this will be, to a large extent, underpinning your success. Your imagination will be stimulated by this planet, with many incredible new and exciting ideas coming to mind.

Mercury and the number 5 are considered somewhat indecisive. Be firm in your attitude and don't let too many ideas or opportunities distract and confuse you. By all means get as much information as you can to help you make the right decisions.

I see you involved with money proposals, job applications, even contracts that need to be signed, so remain as clear-headed as possible.

Your business skills and clear and concise communication will be at the heart of your life in 2010.

Love and pleasure

Mercury, which rules the signs of Gemini and Virgo, will make your love life a little difficult due to its changeable nature. On the one hand you'll feel passionate and loving to your partner, yet on the other you will feel like giving it all up for the excitement of a new affair. Maintain the middle ground.

Also, try not to be too critical with your friends and family members. The influence of Virgo makes you prone to expecting much more from others than they're capable of giving. Control your sharp tongue and don't hurt people's feelings. Encouraging others is the better path, leading to greater emotional satisfaction.

Work

Speed will dominate your professional life in 2010. You'll be flitting from one subject to another and taking on far more than you can handle. You'll need to make some serious changes in your routine to handle the avalanche of work that will come your way. You'll also be travelling with your work, but not necessarily overseas.

If you're in a job you enjoy then this year will give you additional successes. If not, it may be time to move on.

Improving your luck

Communication is the key to attaining your desires in the coming twelve months. Keep focused on one idea rather than scattering your energies in all directions and your success will be speedier.

By looking after your health, sleeping well and exercising regularly, you'll build up your resilience and mental strength.

The 1st, 8th, 15th and 20th hours of Wednesday are lucky so it's best to schedule your meetings and other important social engagements during these times. The lucky numbers for Mercury are 5, 14, 23 and 32.

6 is the year of Venus

Overview

Because you're ruled by 6 this year, love is in the air! Venus, Taurus and Libra are well known for

VIRGO

their affinity with romance, love, and even marriage. If ever you were going to meet a soulmate and feel comfortable in love, 2010 must surely be your year.

Taurus has a strong connection to money and practical affairs as well, so finances will also improve if you are diligent about work and security issues.

The important thing to keep in mind this year is that sharing love and making that important soul connection should be kept high on your agenda. This will be an enjoyable period in your life.

Love and pleasure

Romance is the key thing for you this year and your current relationships will become more fulfilling if you happen to be attached. For singles, a 6 year heralds an important meeting that eventually leads to marriage.

You'll also be interested in fashion, gifts, jewellery and all sorts of socialising. It's at one of these social engagements that you could meet the love of your life. Remain available!

Venus is one of the planets that has a tendency to overdo things, so be moderate in your eating and drinking. Try generally to maintain a modest lifestyle.

Work

You'll have a clearer insight into finances and your future security during a number 6 year. Whereas previously you may have had additional expenses and extra distractions, your mind will now be more settled and capable of longer-term planning along these lines.

With the extra cash you might see this year, decorating your home or office will give you a special sort of satisfaction.

Social affairs and professional activities will be strongly linked. Any sort of work-related functions may offer you romantic opportunities as well. On the other hand, be careful not to mix up your workplace relationships with romantic ideals. This could complicate some of your professional activities.

Improving your luck

You'll want more money and a life of leisure and ease in 2010. Keep working on your strengths and eliminate your negative personality traits to create greater luck and harmony in your life.

Moderate all your actions and don't focus exclusively on money and material objects. Feed your spiritual needs as well. By balancing your inner and outer sides you'll see that your romantic and professional lives will be enhanced more easily.

The 1st, 8th, 15th and 20th hours on Fridays will be very lucky for you and new opportunities will arise for you at those times. You can use the numbers 6, 15, 24 and 33 to increase luck in your general affairs.

7 is the year of Neptune
Overview
The last and most evolved sign of the zodiac is

VIRGO

Pisces, which is ruled by Neptune. The number 7 is deeply connected with this zodiac sign and governs you in 2010. Your ideals seem to be clearer and more spiritually orientated than ever before. Your desire to evolve and understand your inner self will be a double-edged sword. It depends on how organised you are as to how well you can use these spiritual and abstract concepts in your practical life.

Your past hurts and deep emotional issues will be dealt with and removed for good, if you are serious about becoming a better human being.

Spend a little more time caring for yourself rather than others, as it's likely some of your friends will drain you of energy with their own personal problems. Of course, you mustn't turn a blind eye to the needs of others, but don't ignore your own personal requirements in the process.

Love and pleasure

Meeting people with similar life views and spiritual aspirations will rekindle your faith in relationships. If you do choose to develop a new romance, make sure there is a clear understanding of the responsibilities of one to the other. Don't get swept off your feet by people who have ulterior motives.

Keep your relationships realistic and see that the most idealistic partnerships must eventually come down to Earth. Deal with the practicalities of life.

Work

This is a year of hard work, but one in which you'll

come to understand the deeper significance of your professional ideals. You may discover a whole new aspect to your career, which involves a more compassionate and self-sacrificing side to your personality.

You'll also find that your way of working will change and you'll be more focused and able to get into the spirit of whatever you do. Finding meaningful work is very likely and therefore this could be a year when money, security, creativity and spirituality overlap to bring you a great sense of personal satisfaction.

Tapping into your greater self through meditation and self-study will bring you great benefits throughout 2010.

Improving your luck

Using self-sacrifice along with discrimination will be an unusual method of improving your luck. The laws of karma state that what you give, you receive in greater measure. This is one of the principal themes for you in 2010.

The 1st, 8th, 15th and 20th hours of Tuesdays are your lucky times. The numbers 7, 16, 25 and 34 should be used to increase your lucky energies.

8 is the year of Saturn

Overview

The earthy and practical sign of Capricorn and its ruler Saturn are intimately linked to the number

VIRGO

8, which rules you in 2010. Your discipline and far-sightedness will help you achieve great things in the coming year. With cautious discernment, slowly but surely you will reach your goals.

It may be that due to the influence of the solitary Saturn, your best work and achievement will be behind closed doors away from the limelight. You mustn't fear this as you'll discover many new things about yourself. You'll learn just how strong you really are.

Love and pleasure

Work will overshadow your personal affairs in 2010, but you mustn't let this erode the personal relationships you have. Becoming a workaholic brings great material successes but will also cause you to become too insular and aloof. Your family members won't take too kindly to you working 100-hour weeks.

Responsibility is one of the key words for this number and you will therefore find yourself in a position of authority that leaves very little time for fun. Try to make the time to enjoy the company of friends and family and by all means schedule time off on the weekends as it will give you the peace of mind you're looking for.

Because of your responsible attitude it will be very hard for you not to assume a greater role in your workplace and this indicates longer working hours with the likelihood of a promotion with equally good remuneration.

Work

Money is high on your agenda in 2010. Number 8 is a good money number according to the Chinese and this year is at last likely to bring you the fruits of your hard labour. You are cautious and resourceful in all your dealings and will not waste your hard-earned savings. You will also be very conscious of using your time wisely.

You will be given more responsibilities and you're likely to take them on, if only to prove to yourself that you can handle whatever life dishes up.

Expect a promotion in which you'll play a leading role in your work. Your diligence and hard work will pay off, literally, in a bigger salary and more respect from others.

Improving your luck

Caution is one of the key characteristics of the number 8 and is linked to Capricorn. But being overly cautious could cause you to miss valuable opportunities. If an offer is put to you, try to think outside the square and balance it with your naturally cautious nature.

Be gentle and kind to yourself. By loving yourself, others will naturally love you, too. The 1st, 8th, 15th and 20th hours of Saturdays are exceptionally lucky for you, as are the numbers 1, 8, 17, 26 and 35.

VIRGO

9 is the year of Mars

Overview

You are now entering the final year of a nine-year cycle dominated by the planet Mars and the sign of Aries. You'll be completing many things and are determined to be successful after several years of intense work.

Some of your relationships may now have reached their use-by date and even personal affairs may need to be released. Don't let arguments and disagreements get in the road of friendly resolution in these areas of your life.

Mars is a challenging planet, and this year, although you will be very active and productive, you may find others trying to obstruct the achievement of your goals. As a result you may react strongly to them, thereby creating disharmony in your workplace. Don't be so impulsive or reckless, and generally slow things down. The slower, steadier approach has greater merit this year.

Love and pleasure

If you become too bossy and pushy with friends this year you will just end up pushing them out of your life. It's a year to end certain friendships but by the same token it could be the perfect time to remove conflicts and thereby bolster your love affairs in 2010.

If you're feeling a little irritable and angry with those you love, try getting rid of these negative feelings through some intense, rigorous sports and physical activity. This will definitely relieve tension and improve your personal life.

Work

Because you're healthy and able to work at a more intense pace you'll achieve an incredible amount in the coming year. Overwork could become a problem if you're not careful.

Because the number 9 and Mars are infused with leadership energy, you'll be asked to take the reins of the job and steer your company or group in a certain direction. This will bring with it added responsibility but also a greater sense of purpose for you.

Improving your luck

Because of the hot and restless energy of the number 9, it is important to create more mental peace in your life this year. Lower the temperature, so to speak, and decompress your relationships rather than becoming aggravated. Try to talk with your work partners and loved ones rather than telling them what to do. This will generally pick up your health and your relationships.

The 1st, 8th, 15th and 20th hours of Tuesdays are the luckiest for you this year and, if you're involved in any disputes or need to attend to health issues, these times are also very good to get the best results. Your lucky numbers are 9, 18, 27 and 36

VIRGO

2010:
Your Daily Planner

2010: YOUR DAILY PLANNER

Years teach us more than books.

—Berthold Auerbach

According to astrology, the success of any venture or activity is dependent upon the planetary positions at the time you commence that activity. Electional astrology helps you select the most appropriate times for many of your day-to-day endeavours. These dates are applicable to each and every zodiac sign and can be used freely by one and all, even if your star sign doesn't fall under the one mentioned in this book. Please note that the daily planner is a universal system applicable equally to all *twelve* star signs. Anyone and everyone can use this planner irrespective of their birth sign.

Ancient astrologers understood the planetary patterns and how they impacted on each of us. This allowed them to suggest the best possible times to start various important activities. For example, many farmers still use this approach today: they understand the phases of the Moon, and attest to the fact that planting seeds on certain lunar days produces a far better crop than does planting on other days.

In the following section, many facets of daily life are considered. Using the lunar cycle and the combined strength of other planets allows us to work out the best times to do them. This is your personal almanac, which can be used in conjunction with any star sign to help optimise the results.

First, select the activity you are interested in, and then quickly scan the year for the best months to start it. When you have selected the month, you can finetune your timing by finding the best specific dates. You can then be sure that the planetary energies will be in sync with you, offering you the best possible outcome.

Coupled with what you know about your monthly and weekly trends, the daily planner is an effective tool to help you capitalise on opportunities that come your way this year.

Good luck, and may the planets bless you with great success, fortune and happiness in 2010!

Getting started in 2010

How many times have you made a new year's resolution to begin a diet or be a better person in your relationships? And, how many times has it not worked out? Well, part of the reason may be that you started out at the wrong time, because how successful you are is strongly influenced by the position of the Moon and the planets when you begin a particular activity. You will be more successful with the following endeavours if you start them on the days indicated.

Relationships

We all feel more empowered on some days than on others. This is because the planets have some power over us—their movement and their relationships to each other determine the ebb and flow of our energies. And, our levels of self-confidence and sense of romantic magnetism play an important part in the way we behave in relationships.

Your daily planner tells you the ideal dates for meeting new friends, initiating a love affair, spending time with family and loved ones—it even tells you the most appropriate times for sexual encounters.

You'll be surprised at how much more impact you will make in your relationships when you tune yourself in to the planetary energies on these special dates.

Falling in love/restoring love

During these times you could expect favourable energies to meet your soulmate or, if you've had difficulty in a relationship, to approach the one you love to rekindle both your and their emotional responses:

January	18, 20, 23, 24
February	15, 16, 20, 24
March	29
April	16
May	14, 17, 18, 19, 20, 23
June	14, 15, 16, 20, 21
July	12
August	10, 13, 14
September	9, 21, 22
October	8, 18, 19, 20
November	14, 15, 16, 19, 20, 21
December	13, 17, 18

VIRGO

Special times with friends and family

Socialising, partying and having a good time with those whose company you enjoy is highly favourable under the following dates. They are excellent to spend time with family and loved ones in a domestic environment:

January	6, 26, 27
February	12, 13, 14, 15, 16, 20, 24
March	11, 21, 22, 29, 30, 31
April	8
May	15, 16, 17, 18, 19, 20, 23, 24
June	1, 2, 3, 11, 12, 14, 15, 16, 20, 21, 29, 30
July	8, 9, 12, 17, 18, 26, 27
August	5, 6, 9, 10, 13, 14, 22, 23, 24
September	1, 2, 5, 9, 10, 18, 19, 20, 30
October	3, 19, 20, 25, 26, 30, 31
November	3, 4, 14, 15, 16, 22, 26, 27
December	2, 9, 10, 11, 19, 20, 24, 25

Healing or resuming relationships

If you're trying to get back together with the one you love or need a heart-to-heart or deep-and-meaningful discussion with someone, you can try the following dates to do so:

January	12, 13, 14, 15, 21, 22, 23, 24, 25
February	6
March	6, 31
April	2, 7, 8, 12, 16, 19, 23, 24, 25, 26

May	10, 11, 12, 13, 14, 15, 16, 17, 18, 19, 20, 21, 22, 23, 24, 25, 26, 27, 28, 30
June	3, 8, 9, 10, 11, 12, 13, 14, 15, 16, 17, 21, 22, 23, 25, 26, 27, 28, 29, 30
July	1, 2, 3, 4, 5, 10, 11, 12, 13, 15, 16, 17, 18, 19, 20, 21, 22, 23, 28, 29, 30
August	1, 2, 3, 4, 5, 6, 9, 10, 13, 14, 15, 16, 20, 23, 25, 26, 27
September	2, 5, 9, 10, 13, 17, 18, 19, 20
October	1, 2, 3, 6, 12, 13, 14, 15, 20, 22, 23, 24, 25, 26, 27, 28, 29, 30, 31
November	3, 4, 5, 6, 7, 8, 9, 21, 27, 28, 29, 30
December	2, 3, 4, 6, 12, 13, 14, 17, 18, 19, 20, 21, 23, 24, 25

Sexual encounters

Physical and sexual energies are well favoured on the following dates. The energies of the planets enhance your moments of intimacy during these times:

January	1, 6, 7, 21, 22
February	6, 12, 13, 14, 20, 24
March	14, 15, 17, 18, 19, 30, 31
April	23, 24, 25, 26
May	9, 12, 14, 17, 18, 19, 20
June	3, 8, 9, 10, 11, 14, 15, 16, 20, 21, 29, 30
July	8, 9, 10, 11, 12
August	6, 10, 13, 14, 22, 23, 24

VIRGO

September	3, 4, 5, 6, 9, 10, 18, 19, 20, 21, 22, 30
October	1, 2, 3, 7, 8, 18, 19, 20, 23, 24, 28, 29, 30, 31
November	3, 4, 14, 15, 16, 19, 24, 25, 26, 27
December	2, 10, 11, 12, 13, 15, 16, 17, 19, 20, 22, 23, 24, 25

Health and wellbeing

Your aura and life force are susceptible to the movements of the planets—in particular, they respond to the phases of the Moon.

The following dates are the most appropriate times to begin a diet, have cosmetic surgery, or seek medical advice. They also indicate the best times to help others.

Feeling of wellbeing

Your physical as well as your mental alertness should be strong on these following dates. You can plan your activities and expect a good response from others:

January	2, 3, 4, 5, 6, 7, 11, 12, 13, 14, 16, 17, 18, 21, 22, 23, 24, 30, 31
February	1, 2, 7, 8, 15, 16, 17, 18, 19, 20, 21, 22, 23, 24, 25, 26, 27, 28
March	16, 17, 18, 19, 20, 22, 23, 24, 25, 26, 27, 28, 29
April	7, 13, 14, 16, 28
May	2, 11, 14, 25, 26
June	8, 22, 23, 26, 27, 28, 29, 30

July	4, 5, 8, 9, 12, 13, 14, 15, 16, 19, 20, 23, 24, 25
August	5, 6, 9, 10, 11, 12, 13, 15, 16, 20, 21
September	9, 10, 11, 12, 13, 16, 17, 21, 22, 24, 25, 28, 29, 30
October	3, 4, 5, 6, 7, 8, 9, 10, 13, 14, 15, 22
November	4, 5, 6, 10, 11, 19, 20, 21
December	7, 8, 17, 18, 28, 29

Healing and medicine

These times are good for approaching others who have expertise when you need some deeper understanding. They are also favourable for any sort of healing or medication and making appointments with doctors or psychologists. Planning surgery around these dates should bring good results.

Often giving up our time and energy to assist others doesn't necessarily result in the expected outcome. However, by lending a helping hand to a friend on the following dates, the results should be favourable:

January	1, 2, 3, 4, 6, 7, 8, 9, 11, 12, 13, 14, 15, 16, 17, 18, 19, 20, 21, 22, 23, 24, 26, 27, 28, 29, 30, 31
February	1, 5, 6, 9, 11, 12, 13, 14, 15, 16, 19
March	1, 2, 3, 4, 5, 8, 9, 10, 11, 12, 18, 19, 24, 25, 29
April	1, 3, 4, 5, 22, 26
May	4, 5

VIRGO

June	1, 2, 3, 9, 10, 17, 18, 22, 23, 24, 25, 29, 30
July	6, 7, 15, 16, 17, 18, 19, 21, 22, 23, 24, 25, 26
August	2, 3, 4, 11, 12, 17, 18, 19, 20, 21, 30, 31
September	6, 7, 8, 10, 11, 12, 13, 14, 15, 16, 17, 18, 26, 27, 28, 29
October	5, 7, 8, 9, 10, 11, 12, 13, 14, 15, 16, 17, 18, 19, 20, 21, 22, 23, 24, 25, 26, 28, 29, 30, 31
November	1, 2, 3, 5, 7, 8, 10, 11, 14, 15, 17, 18, 19, 22, 23
December	4, 5, 7, 8, 9, 10, 12, 13, 14, 16, 23, 24, 25, 26, 28, 29, 30, 31

Money

Money is an important part of life, and involves many decisions—decisions about borrowing, investing, spending. The ideal times for transactions are very much influenced by the planets, and whether your investment or nest egg grows or doesn't grow can often be linked to timing. Making your decisions on the following dates could give you a whole new perspective on your financial future.

Managing wealth and money

To build your nest egg it's a good time to open your bank account or invest money on the following dates:

January	1, 6, 7, 13, 14, 15, 18, 21, 22, 28, 29
February	3, 4, 9, 10, 11, 12, 13, 14, 15, 17, 18, 24, 25
March	2, 3, 9, 10, 16, 17, 18, 23, 24, 29, 30, 31
April	5, 6, 7, 13, 14, 19, 20, 21, 26, 27,

May	2, 3, 4, 10, 11, 17, 18, 23, 24, 30, 31
June	6, 7, 8, 13, 14, 19, 20, 21, 26, 27, 28
July	4, 5, 10, 11, 12, 17, 18, 23, 24, 25, 31
August	1, 7, 8, 13, 14, 20, 21, 27, 28, 29
September	3, 4, 9, 10, 16, 17, 23, 24, 25
October	1, 2, 7, 8, 13, 14, 15, 21, 22, 28, 29
November	3, 4, 10, 11, 17, 18, 24, 25
December	1, 2, 7, 8, 14, 15, 16, 21, 22, 23, 24, 29

Spending

It's always fun to spend but the following dates are more in tune with this activity and are likely to give you better results:

January	3, 4, 5, 6, 7, 8, 9, 10, 11, 12, 13, 14
February	3, 4, 5, 10, 19
March	8, 10, 11, 13, 14, 19
April	7, 8, 11, 12, 22
May	6, 7, 8, 9, 10, 11, 12, 13, 17, 18, 19, 20, 21, 22, 23, 24, 25, 26, 27, 28
June	1, 11, 12, 14, 16, 17, 19, 23, 25, 26, 27, 28, 29, 30
July	6, 7, 8, 23, 24, 25, 26, 27, 28, 29, 31
August	1, 2, 3, 4, 5, 15, 16, 17, 18, 19, 30, 31
September	1, 2, 3, 4, 17, 18, 19, 20, 21, 22, 23, 27, 28, 29, 30
October	4, 7, 12, 13, 14, 15, 16, 17, 18, 19, 27, 28
November	2, 3, 4, 25, 26, 27, 28
December	11, 22, 23

VIRGO

Selling

If you're thinking of selling something, whether it is small or large, consider the following dates as ideal times to do so:

January	18
February	12, 13, 14, 15
March	5, 6, 9, 14, 15, 16, 17, 18, 19, 21
April	1, 3, 4, 5, 22, 26
May	7, 12, 21, 29
June	3, 8, 9, 10, 11, 12, 13, 17, 24, 25, 26, 27, 28, 30
July	1, 2, 7, 9, 10, 11, 25, 27, 28, 29, 30, 31
August	1, 2, 3, 4, 5, 6, 7, 8, 9, 10, 13, 20, 23, 28
September	2, 9, 10, 11, 12, 13, 14, 15, 16, 17, 18, 19, 20, 21, 22, 23, 24, 26, 30
October	1, 2, 3, 4, 6, 7, 10, 11, 17, 18, 19, 20, 21, 22, 23, 24, 25, 27, 29
November	3, 4, 5, 6, 7, 11, 14, 15, 16, 17, 18, 19, 21, 23, 24, 25, 26, 27, 28, 29, 30
December	1, 2, 3, 4, 5, 6, 7, 8, 9, 10, 11, 12, 13, 14, 15, 16, 17, 18, 19, 20, 21, 22

Borrowing

Few of us like to borrow money, but if you must, taking out a loan on the following dates will be positive:

January	12, 30
February	7, 12, 13
March	6, 7, 8, 11
April	3, 4, 8
May	9, 28, 29
June	1, 2, 3, 4, 5, 29, 30
July	1, 2, 3, 26, 27, 28, 29, 30
August	9, 25, 26
September	5, 6
October	3, 30
November	26, 27
December	3, 4, 21, 22, 23, 30, 31

Work and education

Your career is important, and continual improvement of your skills is therefore also crucial professionally, mentally and socially. The dates below will help you find out the most appropriate times to improve your professional talents and commence new work or education associated with your work.

You may need to decide when to start learning a new skill, when to ask for a promotion, and even when to make an important career change. Here are the days when your mental and educational power is strong.

VIRGO

Learning new skills

Educational pursuits are lucky and bring good results on the following dates:

January	15, 16, 17, 18, 19, 20, 21, 22, 25, 26, 27
February	14, 15, 16, 17, 18, 19, 22, 23, 28
March	16, 17, 18, 21, 22, 27, 28
April	17, 18, 24, 25
May	15, 16, 21, 22
June	12, 17, 18, 24, 25
July	15, 16, 21, 22, 23, 24, 25
August	11, 12, 17, 18, 19
September	8, 13, 15, 20, 21, 22
October	11, 12
November	7, 8, 9
December	6, 19, 20

Changing career path or profession

If you're feeling stuck and need to move into a new professional activity, changing jobs could be done at these times:

January	6, 7, 15, 16, 17, 23, 24
February	12, 13, 14, 19, 20, 21
March	19, 20, 27, 28
April	15, 16, 24, 25
May	14, 21, 22
June	17, 18, 19, 20, 21
July	8, 9, 15, 16, 23, 24, 25

August	5, 6, 11, 12, 20, 21, 22, 23
September	1, 2, 8, 13, 14, 15, 17
October	8, 13, 14, 15, 16, 17
November	3, 4, 10, 11, 19, 20, 21
December	1, 2, 3, 7, 8, 17, 18, 28, 29

Promotion, professional focus and hard work

To increase your mental focus and achieve good results from the work you do; promotions are also likely on these dates:

January	4, 5, 6, 11, 12, 13, 14, 15, 16, 17, 18, 19, 21
February	6
March	16, 17, 18, 19, 20, 21, 23, 24, 25, 26, 27, 28, 29
April	8, 28, 29
May	12, 21
June	25, 26, 27, 28
July	4, 5, 8, 9, 12, 13, 14, 15, 16, 17, 18, 19, 20, 21, 22, 23, 24, 25, 26, 27
August	5, 6, 10, 11, 12, 13, 14, 15, 16, 17, 18, 19, 20, 21, 22, 23, 24
September	13, 14, 15
October	10, 11, 12, 13, 14, 15, 17, 18, 19, 20, 22, 23, 24, 30, 31
November	2, 4, 5, 6, 7, 8, 9, 23, 24, 25, 26, 27, 28, 29, 30
December	2, 3, 4, 11, 12, 13, 14, 15, 16, 18, 19, 20, 21, 23, 24, 25

Travel

Setting out on a holiday or adventurous journey is exciting. Here are the most favourable times for doing this. Travel on the following dates is likely to give you a sense of fulfilment:

January	15
February	15, 16, 18, 19, 20, 21
March	16, 17, 18, 21, 22, 23
April	19, 24, 25, 26, 27
May	16, 17, 18, 21, 22
June	17, 18, 19, 20, 21, 24, 25
July	21, 22, 23, 24, 25
August	19
September	9, 21, 22
October	18, 19, 20, 21, 22
November	7, 16, 17, 18
December	6, 14, 16, 19, 20

Beauty and grooming

Believe it or not, cutting your hair or nails has a powerful effect on your body's electromagnetic energy. If you cut your hair or nails at the wrong time of the month, you can reduce your level of vitality significantly. Use these dates to ensure you optimise your energy levels by staying in tune with the stars.

Hair and nails

January	1, 2, 3, 4, 5, 6, 7, 8, 11, 12, 13, 14, 15, 18, 19, 20, 21, 22, 25, 26, 27
February	3, 4, 5, 7, 8, 15, 16, 17, 18, 19, 22, 23, 24, 25
March	2, 3, 4, 6, 7, 8, 14, 15, 21, 22
April	1, 2, 3, 4, 5, 10, 11, 12, 17, 18, 19, 20, 21, 22, 23, 28, 29, 30
May	1, 2, 3, 4, 5, 7, 8, 9, 10, 11, 12, 13, 15, 16, 17, 18, 25, 26 27, 28, 29, 30
June	4, 5, 11, 12, 14, 15, 16, 24, 25
July	1, 2, 3, 8, 9, 12, 13, 14, 21, 22, 28, 29, 30
August	1, 2, 5, 6, 17, 18, 19, 25, 26
September	1, 2, 6, 7, 14, 15, 21, 22, 23, 24, 28, 29, 30
October	3, 4, 11, 12, 18, 19, 20, 25, 26, 27, 28, 29, 30
November	7, 8, 9, 14, 15, 16, 22, 23, 24, 25, 26, 27
December	5, 6, 12, 13, 19, 20, 21, 22, 23, 24, 25

Therapies, massage and self-pampering

January	6, 7, 13, 14, 15, 18, 19, 20, 21
February	2, 3, 9, 11, 14
March	1, 9, 14, 16, 17, 20, 23, 29
April	4, 5, 6, 10, 11, 12, 13, 17, 25, 26
May	2, 3, 7, 8, 9, 10, 11, 14, 15, 16, 17, 22, 23, 24, 31
June	3, 5, 12, 18, 19, 26, 27
July	4, 7, 8, 9, 10, 16, 23, 28, 29, 30, 31
August	3, 4, 5, 6, 7, 13, 20, 21, 24, 25, 26, 27, 28, 31
September	2, 17, 21, 28, 29

VIRGO

October	13, 14, 15, 18, 19, 21, 25, 26, 27, 28
November	2, 3, 9, 11, 14, 15, 16, 17, 21, 24, 29
December	7, 12, 13, 14, 15, 18, 19, 20, 22, 26, 27, 28, 29

MILLS & BOON
MODERN

...International affairs, seduction and passion guaranteed

The Playboy of Pengarroth Hall
Susanne James

Constantine's Defiant Mistress
Sharon Kendrick

10 brand-new titles each month

5 available on the first Friday of every month and
5 available on the third Friday of every month from
WHSmith, ASDA, Tesco, Eason
and all good bookshops
Also available as eBooks
www.millsandboon.co.uk

MILLS & BOON
ROMANCE

Pure romance, pure emotion

Two 2-in-1 anthologies each month

Available on the first Friday of every month
from WHSmith, ASDA, Tesco, Eason
and all good bookshops
Also available as eBooks
www.millsandboon.co.uk

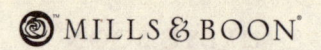

MILLS & BOON
Historical

Rich, vivid and passionate

4 brand-new titles each month

Available on the first Friday of every month
from WHSmith, ASDA, Tesco, Eason
and all good bookshops
Also available as eBooks
www.millsandboon.co.uk

MILLS & BOON
MEDICAL™

*Pulse-raising romance –
Heart-racing medical drama*

MILLS & BOON
HOT-SHOT SURGEON, CINDERELLA BRIDE
Alison Roberts
THE PLAYBOY DOCTOR CLAIMS HIS BRIDE
Janice Lynn
MEDICAL™ 2-in-1

MILLS & BOON
EMERGENCY: WIFE LOST AND FOUND
Carol Marinelli

6 brand-new stories each month
Two 2-in-1s and two individual titles

Available on the first Friday of every month
from WHSmith, ASDA, Tesco, Eason
and all good bookshops
Also available as eBooks
www.millsandboon.co.uk

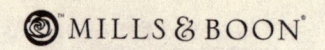

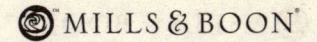

MILLS & BOON
SPECIAL MOMENTS

A lifetime of love grows from shared moments

TRUSTING RYAN
Tara Taylor Quinn
THE BACHELOR'S STAND-IN WIFE
Susan Crosby

FAMILY IN PROGRESS
Brenda Harlen

10 brand-new stories each month
Three 2-in-1s and four individual titles

Available on the third Friday of every month
from WHSmith, ASDA, Tesco, Eason
and all good bookshops
Also available as eBooks
www.millsandboon.co.uk

⬥ MILLS & BOON
INTRIGUE

Breathtaking romance & adventure

9 brand-new stories each month
Three 2-in-1s and three individual titles

Available on the first and third Friday of every month
from WHSmith, ASDA, Tesco, Eason
and all good bookshops
Also available as eBooks
www.millsandboon.co.uk

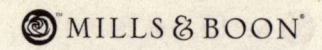